Day Trading For Beginners

Day Trading Secrets For Beginner's

By: Priyank Gala

Published By:

Priyank Gala

©Copyright 2015 – : Priyank Gala

ISBN-13: 978-1517565404
ISBN-10: 1517565405

Table of Contents

Chapter 1: What is Day Trading?

   Day Trading and Its Advantages

Chapter 2: Avoiding Pitfalls - Important Rules in Day Trading

Chapter 3: Understanding Price Movement

Chapter 4: Technical Indicators

   Moving Averages

   Bollinger Bands and Keltner Channels

   Strength Indicators

Chapter 5: Analyzing List of Stocks

Chapter 6: Rules in Trading

CHAPTER 7: UNDERSTANDING VOLUMES AND THEIR SIGNIFICANCE

CHAPTER 8: Understanding Market Technique

CHAPTER 9: Dull Markets and the Opportunities They Bring

Chapter 10: Strategies on Effective Day Trading to Live By

Chapter 11: Day Trading for Beginners, its Do's and Don'ts

Chapter 1: What is Day Trading?

As the name implies, day trading happens in one trading day wherein activities such as acquiring and selling of various financial instruments occur. Day traders, otherwise known as active traders, are the type of individuals who perform day trading. At first glance, day trading may seem like a decent and exciting job. Just like any other trading ventures, one must have a good overall understanding of its various aspects in order to succeed.

If day trading sparks one's interest, one of the first things that should be understood are the several types of financial instruments that are being used in trading. These would include interest rate futures, currencies, stocks, and stock options, among others.

Apart from making one's self-familiar with the needed financial instruments, the person should also consider studying relevant strategies in day trading in order to be assured that one will not feel lost in the process. One must remember that there are other things that are involved in day trading apart from merely purchasing financial instruments. In reality, it can be complicated which makes it important for a potential day trader to be committed and focused so as to achieve success in venturing into something new.

Day Trading and Its Advantages

Professional traders who used to monopolize stock trading are now a thing of the past. These days, everybody can come and trade as they want. Such is one big advantage when doing day trading. The line that distinguishes amateurs from professionals is no longer recognized.

Day trading, as a whole, is anybody's ball game, as long as you possess the right system in place and understand well when is the best time to execute.

- The first advantage of day trading that one should understand is SPEED. Current traders can take advantage of the state of the art technology being used these days since it allows them to receive and analyze real-time price quotes and send an execution order directly to the NASDAQ market maker via electronic means. Since every confirmation is done in a span of seconds, traders can easily opt out as soon as they want to if they believe they already have what they want.
- The second advantage is OPTIMAL CONTROL. Day trading makes yourself as your own boss and, therefore, you are not obliged to respond to anyone since you are your own broker. Decisions such as purchasing,

selling, analyzing trends or scrutinizing the current financial data are all done by you. Moreover, you need not worry about price slippage since market prices are constantly monitored. Whenever you are trading, you are always aware when is the best bidding time or what is the best asking price.

- The third advantage is A GOOD NIGHT'S SLEEP. Yes, you heard it right. A good night's sleep is what you can get because you would constantly go home flat. Furthermore, there is no such thing as overnight position which minimizes the risk of exposure, something that usually happens overnight.

Being a day trader means that you know the risk you could face, you are ready to take a chance which depends on the signs and signals that you're reading and then you hope that your system is not faulty. On certain occasions when the system fails to work, you would calmly tell yourself that you believe you did your best, gather your losses, and decide in the end to leave. Otherwise, if you have placed your trust on someone else to do the trading and that person is not doing what he is expected to do while being a pain in the ass during the whole process, you may think about aiming a rifle against your head. Why? Simple. You don't know who to actually put the blame on – the mediocre broker or yourself – for letting him throw your money down the drain right before your eyes.

Understanding well the advantages of being a day trader should be able to encourage more individuals to participate in an industry that is once considered as "restricted." On the other hand, it should also be remembered that it doesn't really look easy as it sounds. One must realize that he needs to be equipped with the right education if he wants to make it big. Luckily, there are a number of online resources available for anyone who wants to upgrade his skills or learn new tricks of the trade.

Courses on day trading should be able to help you a lot in making good decisions when you are purchasing and selling. If, by chance, you see some software that claims it can do all the thinking on your behalf, ignore it. Moreover, find the time to join forums and never hesitate to seek advice from professional traders. Those who are considered as seasoned traders would be more than willing to act as your mentor. You can absolutely learn a lot from their experiences in order to determine the best strategies that you can use according to your favor. Additionally, you should take note of the worst decisions they have made which led them to their biggest downfall and remember not to repeat them.

When you are doing these things long enough, you will soon find yourself trading with ease and be able to sometimes predict the next thing that is bound to happen according to the trends. You should be able to learn how to read the signals and use your guts to proceed with what you believe is right. Being a day trader also means you have no one else to rely on but yourself.

Since you are a newbie in the exciting world of day trading, you should familiarize yourself with its do's and don't's. Just like any other kinds of the new venture, you can't proceed with day trading when you are walking on thin ice. You need to equip yourself with a good load of knowledge.

Chapter 2: Avoiding Pitfalls - Important Rules in Day Trading

If you depend only on technical analysis, chart patterns, risk management, or marketing strategies, you may not be able to last long in the industry. You should take the extra mile and move beyond the technical side of day trading in order to earn consistent optimum results. One thing that most people don't understand is that this should be treated like a profession, that for one to stay ahead, one needs to exert some level of effort to move further than the learning phase. Apart from this, one must also take note of other important trading rules in order to prevent pitfalls.

The worst mistake that one can commit is when they think about joining day trading as something similar to joining the lottery, that is, waiting for a miracle to happen and reaping a treasure chest full of money. However, things don't work in such way. What a person needs to have is the right level of attitude, discipline and self-control for him to succeed and not merely survive. No matter how many books you've read about learning the ins and outs of the stock market and gathering all your resources online along with joining forums in order to gain useful insight on the rules and strategies of day trading, you will get nothing if you don't know how to hit the perfect balance between using your thoughts and relying on your emotions.

The following are some useful day trading rules that can be followed by both tyros and pros:

Be Sure to Have a Consistent Frame of Mind

You need to know that the market, being in a highly volatile environment, should not be seen as a consistent industry. In other words, things don't usually turn out the way you want them to be. The secret lies in being able to adapt, think fast, and doing the right moves to avoid being left behind. You should be able to read the probability scenario as this will surely bring some leverage. As soon as you've mastered how to deal with these probability set-ups, you would be able to determine the perfect timing on when to perform trading.

Keep Your Cool, Remember Not To Overtrade

This type of mistake is common among beginners. You should be able to know how to keep your cool and avoid getting too excited in order not to commit the gravest sins in trading. You should also know how to be patient and be willing to wait until you feel absolutely sure that the right time for you to strike has come. The way you control yourself can greatly affect your gains and losses.

Learn How to Focus To Avoid Getting Derailed

It's true that in day trading, everybody understands that there are risks involved and that large amounts of money are at stake. The truth is, these risks can be considered as minimal if the person can follow time-tested rules in trading. There's nothing wrong when you shift gears from time to time as a way to find out if you can also follow what the successful pros are doing. However, this should be done not too often. Be reminded that these pros have been in the business for years, and they can always see the bigger picture. In your case, you should know that the more often you try to experiment, the more money you would lose in the process.

Don't Ever Force Yourself Into Trading If Your Mind Is Not Ready

Making instantaneous decisions can be difficult if your mind is not in a good state, you lack sleep or you are suffering from an anxiety attack. Simply speaking, it's not all worth the risk. Remember that you can trade only if you are physically, mentally and emotionally ready to do so.

Use a Trading Log to Your Advantage

Most traders see this as something that is unnecessary but they are mistaken. Not only is it important to log every trade, it is also necessary to write down your thoughts and emotions while doing the entire process of trading. What you can do is make a comparison between your wins and your losses. Analyze the state of mind you have when you were winning. Likewise, what do you think have been eating you emotionally or have been troubling your thoughts when you were having all these losses? Finding answers to these questions will allow you to have a better idea of what you should do the next time. The truth is, there no single perfect strategy that can be used by everybody. Knowing how to come up with the most useful trading rules that can bring the most benefit is a skill that every trader ought to know.

Chapter 3: Understanding Price Movement

Always be reminded that the stock market moves incessantly. Prices move up, and they also move down. This is the same with individual stocks. Prices also move downward and upward. Don't ever think that just because the market overall is moving up, any other stock will follow the upward trend. Such notion is not true. The stock market, in reality, is filled with thousands of individual stocks. That means when you hear the phrase "the market is up," the average of all involved stocks in that aggregate is heading up. However, there are some exceptions that should be considered. You should know that the market may be favorable to financial stocks at a time and then become favorable to retail stocks the next. Then, when the market is in favor of retail stocks overall, it is highly likely that it will be in favor of some more than others. Some of those retail stock will be dropping, some will be rising. In this chapter, we will have a closer look at price movement. You should be able to have a good understanding why prices change in order to have a solid foundation for everything else that you need to be doing.

The next question is: What creates price movement that is found in individual stocks? There are several possible answers. First and foremost, let's discuss the overall market. All stocks are traded within the overall stock market environment. While it is possible to trade an individual stock with no regard to this concept, it should be noted that results can actually improve if the individual is very much aware of this market environment. Investor concerns such as military involvement in a different country, the debate in Washington on the debt ceiling, China manufacturing, employment, etc. can widely cause the overall stock market to become higher or lower on any given day. Some things can actually influence market sentiment. You should always make yourself aware of the news and economic reports that are said to bring influence to investor sentiment.

Let us now focus our discussion on individual stocks. What can cause them to move up or to move down?

1. The truth is, the overall market sentiment can leave an impact. If we notice that the whole market is moving up, then we get the notion that the market sentiment is bullish as prices are moving up. If we see that the whole market is moving down, then we can say that market sentiment is bearish. This brings us to the idea that the price of an individual stock tends to move higher for the simple reason that the

overall sentiment among investors is bullish which in the end causes investors to purchase stocks. If by chance you are pondering on buying Apple stock (ticker symbol AAPL), and then the overall market sentiment gives a bullish picture, you may then decide to go ahead and place such buy today. As the old adage goes, "bulls rush in."

2. Quarterly reports are in fact issued by all those companies that are listed among the major U.S. stock exchanges. Such reports are essential in order to be listed on such types of exchanges, allowing investors to know the health conditions of the companies they are intending to place their investments in. Some of the things that are included in these reports are profit, sales growth and earnings. In other words, if a company reports some good news, do you think that their share price would also go up? If you answer yes, you are absolutely correct.

Here is an example. Zales is a jewelry shop and it has been faced with years of struggle. When the company filed their quarterly report on August 28, 2013, however, it was found out that they had their first profitable year since 2008. Do you think investors find this favorable? Let's look at the chart below.

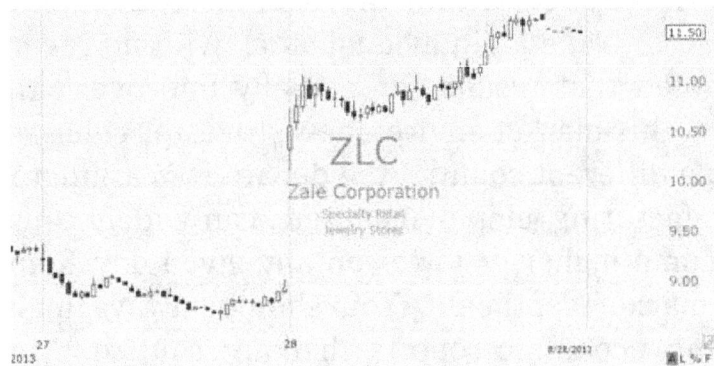

On the above chart, notice how the closing price for Zale Corporation was calculated to fall around $9.00 on the day prior to the release of the report. Then, on the day that the report was released, the price moved up by over 10 percent and it continued to move up from there. Towards the end of the day, the price was seen to have reached more than $11.50 for every share. This is what we can say as a big price move.

Let's pause for a minute at this point. If, for example, you have decided to buy ZLC stock on the 27th, do you think you'd take the chance to sell it when the market opened then likewise take your 10 percent profit? You would probably do this. Some people would surely do so. However, a number of investors believed this was a big deal. For this reason, they decided on buying the stock even though there was an increase in the price by more than 10 percent compared to the previous day.

There are some investors who, after buying the stock on a day, decided to sell it on the same day and treated it like a day trade. It also means that they were able to take their profit on the same trading day. Other investors would decide to buy the stock for the purpose of holding it overnight, thinking that the price would continue to get even higher in the not so distant future. This latter type of traders are what we can call as swing traders because they aim for catching the bigger swings in stock price and would never think about selling it on the same day that they bought it.

Take note that the quarterly reports for companies don't usually show positive news. For example, when ZLC gained a higher jump, that same day, STEEL Manufacturing gained a lower drop.

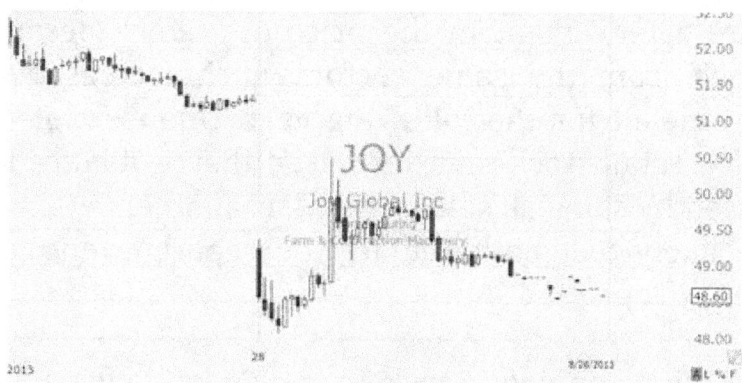

On the chart displayed above, you would see that point where STEEL dropped on August 28, the day when the market opened. While it shows that there is an upward movement, it also shows that it went lower than the closing price of the previous day (shown by the line in yellow). This is because investors are not agreeable to the report.

3. Another reason for a stock price to change is because usually, a change would occur in the C-suite. When there's a sudden departure of a CFO or a CEO, it usually causes the price to plunge down because it gives a sign of possible instability and, therefore, poses a higher risk for investors. However, things happened differently when Steve Ballmer announced

in August (August 23) about his plans to leave his post as the CEO of Microsoft within the following year. Though it's possible that the announcement didn't make him feel any better, it was noted that the stock share price rose dramatically afterward even though the price seemed to have been fading from that point. Let's see how the price moved based on the chart below.

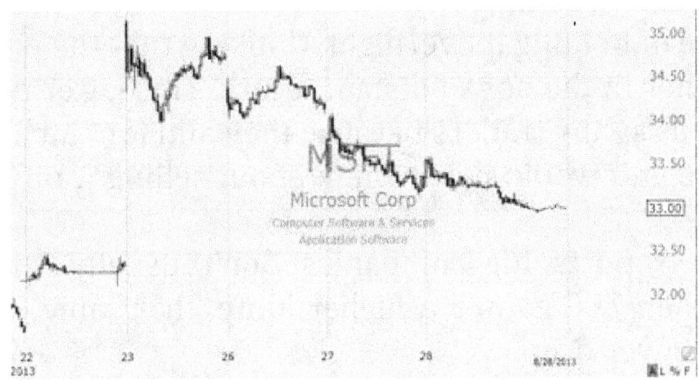

4. We can say that there's a movement in the price of a stock because there's a different stock from the same sector which increased or lowered their guidance meant for the following year. One example of such case is the so-called retail stock that decreased their guidance for the upcoming year caused by sluggish sales. Likewise, another retailer's investors would most likely feel bothered by the report, eventually causing the share price to drop.

5. It is highly likely for a biotechnology stock to move suddenly up or down since it is directly affected by drug trials and approvals made by the FDA.

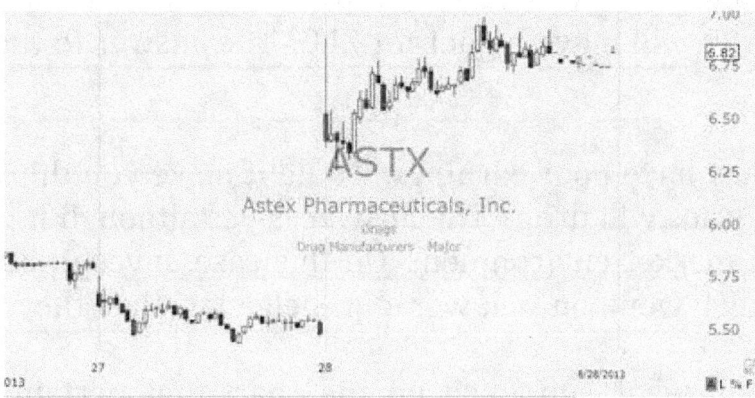

On the chart above, notice how Linden Pharmaceuticals leaped on August 28th after announcing about the successful trial of a new drug during the second phase. In just one day when the news was released, the price jumped to more than 20 percent.

In reality, some reasons can be cited in order to explain why a change can occur in the price. However, the five above-mentioned examples are enough to provide a good sense of price movement.

Let me now show you one last chart before we proceed to probabilities.

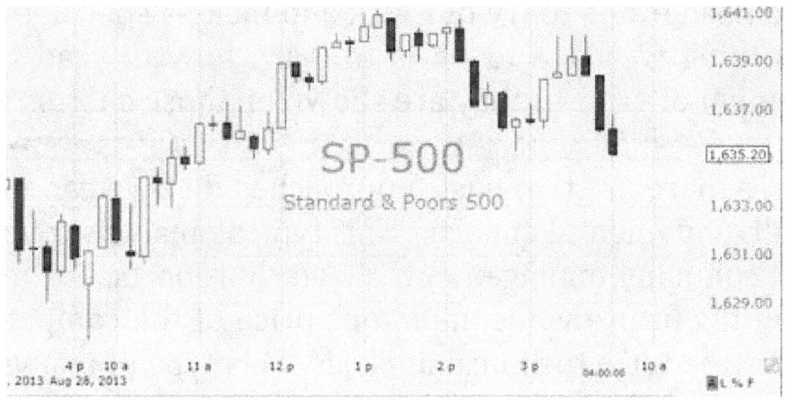

The chart shown above displays the S&P-500 for August 28, 2013. This is the same date that applies to the various individual stock charts. The S&P-500 is a stock index made up of 500 listed stocks on the exchanges which is often regarded as a representative of the bigger market. You can also take note of the NASDAQ Composite and the DJ-30, among others. We are showing this chart to reiterate my earlier statement that all stocks show movement in the same environment of the bigger market.

Let us now discuss some probabilities. If, for example, this day of trading's market environment is bullish and then an announcement on positive earnings was heard from Zale Corporation, would it then lead you to think of a high probability that the price will move higher for ZLC? The answer to this is a resounding yes.

If STEEL announces that they have poor earnings, would it make you think of a high probability that the price will drop? The answer is yes although it may be different with a bullish market environment. On this case, investors may opt to buy on the price that went on a lower dip, believing that they are getting a bargain.

Such situation could explain what happened on the chart that pertains to STEEL. Initially, the price moved lower. Later on, the price moved higher. Do you think the price could have gone up because of a negative market environment? Perhaps no. However, such occurrence, at least, may not be regarded as a high probability situation.

These tasks make up the daily assessment you have to do in your role as a day trader since your desire is to make high probability trades. You have to consider some things such as market probabilities, market psychology, and market sentiment. The good news is that we don't need to guess on all of these things. It is simply because we can see all price changes on the charts right before our eyes. There's no need for us to try our luck and make a speculation on these things. The only thing we have to do is to learn how to read the charts and study the movement of price as they are shown on those charts.

In the stock market analysis, there are two basic approaches that we can use. The first one is what we call fundamental analysis. This type of analysis covers sector strength, dividends, company management, quarterly reports, etc. and gives out an assessment on the future value and stock price of the company. The second one is known by the term technical analysis. This type of analysis believes that all things concerned about the stock value can be wrapped up in the stock's current price. Remember that these two different types of analysis don't have any exclusivity over the other. However, investors would usually lean towards one or the other. In the case of day trading, we will place our emphasis on technical analysis. It may be true that we could be influenced by the laws of probability as based on the various circumstances that were mentioned in the chapter. Then again, we should still consider the price movement that is shown on the charts in order to help us decide on the right time to buy and to sell.

In the next chapter, we shall start to delve deeper into technical analysis and then study in greater detail the price movement on individual stocks. Remember that in day trading, there's no such thing as a hindsight. Minute by minute, we can notice that there's a movement of price as shown on the chart which we can see right before our eyes. Indeed, it's convenient to look simply back at the price of ZLC and watch the price to keep on getting higher. On the other hand when the price changes in every minute, there are some tools that we could use which could aid us in navigating our trading decisions. We should now take a much deeper look into things.

Chapter 4: Technical Indicators

If you intend on using technical indicators when trading in the stock market, you should, therefore, be prepared to become a little bit technical. There's no denying the fact that some area of this stuff can be dull and boring.....unless you start to notice how it actually works. Later on when technical analysis starts to help you gain some money in the stock market, that's when things start to become even more interesting.

One thing that should be remembered about technical indicators is that all of them should be treated as derivatives of price. All of them provide ways of measuring how the price behaves on the chart right before our eyes. In reality, there are hundreds of technical indicators we should take note of. No worries. I'm not in the position to lecture on these hundred technical indicators. There's no need to use that much since doing so can actually distort the idea that all of them are derivatives of price. In other words, every time we use technical indicators, we should always be reminded about one thing: price action is a primal matter. True, it is possible to do some stock trading just by simply looking at the price movement regardless of any indicators involved. However, on the ideal side of it, these indicators will actually help you perform high probability trades. In short, you have the objective to earn a profit by providing a discerning answer to this question: "What should the price be able to do next?"

I know that you are trying to predict on the price movement. Most people won't divulge about this. Instead, they will tell you that you cannot do it. However, this same person will also buy a stock under one price while having the expectation that ....(Can you guess the answer?)... the price will move higher. There's no other way to explain why they are buying it here. So even if they are saying that it is impossible, it could also be safe for us to assume that they can also see the price to have the tendency to go higher. Otherwise, they would never have bought in the first place. So now we are beginning to get the hang of predicting how the price would move in the future.

Do you think we could be correct at all times? The answer is "no." Do you also think that it's important for us to be correct at all times? Again, the answer is "no." This is actually the full picture involved in high probability trading. We are aware of the fact that we don't usually identify correctly the direction where the price is heading. However, by using some good technical analysis, we can gain some edge. Moreover, we can increase the odds that can make the cards stacked according to our favor. If we regularly use the same edge every time that we make a trading decision while at the same time we limit the risk involved when we make a mistake, then we're on our way of creating a high probability trading system. Do you believe this is possible? Of course yes. Do you think this is easy? It is not. Developing a high probability system will need some time. Even mastering its application would need a longer period of time. Chances are, we just tend to get in the way.

Candles

The word "candles" at this part does not literally mean the candle that we light up with a match. It actually refers to the term "price candles" that are used by most day traders on their charts. Just like what I have mentioned earlier, all indicators derive from the price. However, there are some ways to represent the price in the chart. Two of them are known as the primary methods being used. These are the bar charts and the candle charts, otherwise known as candlesticks.

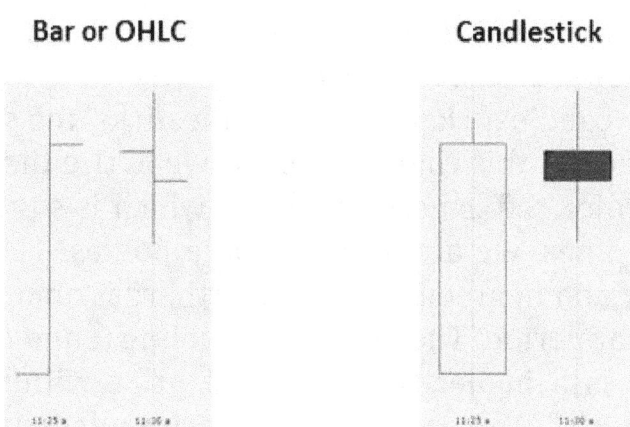

If we need to look at the price action, we should be able to answer these four questions:
1. What was the price at opening?
2. What was the price at closing?
3. What was the high?
4. What was the low?

Answering these questions shall be based on the time frame that we are studying. The next charts tell us that the life of a stock has a period of 10 minutes. Consequently, these 10 minutes are further divided into two prints wherein each one is five minutes. (Notice that each chart has two five-minute candles/bars).

First, let us take a look at the bar chart on the left. Note that the opening price for the 5-minute period is represented by the horizontal line which appears to be sticking out to the left side of the vertical line. The closing price is likewise represented by the horizontal line that appears to be sticking out to the right side of the vertical line. We can see the high by looking at the highest point on the vertical line. The low can then be seen by looking at the lowest point on the vertical line. Now, since we can see that the opening line falls underneath the closing line, we can, therefore, deduce that the price closed higher within a span of five minutes. This explains why the bar is colored green which means that there was a net gain within the period of five minutes.

On the second bar chart, we notice that the opening price is found on top of the closing price and that the line is in red color. The reason for this is that the price closed lower within that period of five minutes.

Let us now shift our focus at the candlestick. In some candlesticks, the simple colors of black and white are used. On this chart, however, we notice the color green is used for up while the color red is used for down which is similar to the bar chart. Instead of seeing lines, we are seeing candle bodies. The first candle body, which looks hollow and in green, tells us that there is an upward movement of the price within that period. The small vertical line found on top of the body tells us that there is a higher movement of price within that period. We call this small line "wick." We can say that the price opened at the base part of the aforementioned body simply because we don't see any line beneath it. This means that for this type of candle, the opening is identical to the base of the candle. By looking at the top of the body, we could then see the closing price.

When we look at the next candlestick, we can see that the candle body is in red and filled. This means that the price closed at a lower rate within that period. On the top part where we can see the wick, it tells us that the price has gone higher within that period while the vertical line found underneath the body tells us that the price had gone lower within that period. There are times when the line, which in this case is found below the body, is called the shadow instead of wick. In my opinion, shadow is a more appropriate term since we usually associate the word "wick" as something that is found on the top part of a candle.

Since we have gathered this basic information on the table, the next thing we need to do is to ask ourselves the question "Why is this important?" Note that every bar or candle gives us the story of price. We also get an insight on how "the market" sees the price at this point of time. When we say "the market," we are actually referring to the other traders who are trading the said stock at this period of time. Some of them are even what we call as "live traders" and they are sitting in homes or offices like everyone else. There are some of them who are institutional traders since they make trades on behalf of a group of other investors. Some traders are what we can call as "computers" because they trade price that is based on programs that had been written by quantitative analysts, otherwise known as "quants." No matter who is making the trade, we can still have an idea on what all of these types of traders think about the price at this point in time.

Again, let's take a look at the candlesticks and figure out what they mean. The first candle tells us that in buying the stock, the investors seemed to have rushed in. These investors were very bullish. We can say this because the candle body is relatively tall as compared to the candles surrounding it. We also notice that it is green and that there is no shadow underneath the body. The second candle tells us that investors seemed to be having some difficulty in making up their mind on the huge run up in price. The reason for this is that perhaps some of the investors who bought prior to the big run up had already begun to take their profit since they notice that the gain was too much and that it happens too fast. This notion can be attributed to the fact that only a few investors intend to get into the trade following a big run up. Probably they are waiting for the price to pull back a little before they decide to buy the stock.

We can see then that the end result of the second candle is that the price had gone lower which is actually all that we need to know. There's even no need to interview everyone who had been involved in this trade by asking them about their thoughts. The candle is enough to give us an idea of everything that we should know. It tells us that at this point in time, a run up seemed too much for this stock. If, for example, investors had the notion that it was still a considerably great deal, the next candle should be tall and green just the same. In this case, it is not since it appears to be down. In your opinion, would you say that this is a great time to decide on buying this stock long? Would you say that there is a high probability that it will go higher?

Looking at just a single candle can already give us some information. When we look at several more candles, however, we also get more information. Based on what we have seen so far, these five-minute candles belong to the chart for STEEL manufacturing that I have shown earlier. Such chart of STEEL tells the story by using 10-minute candles. In the next chart, I am about to show the 5-minute chart and the newly discussed two candles where there is a blue arrow pointing at them.

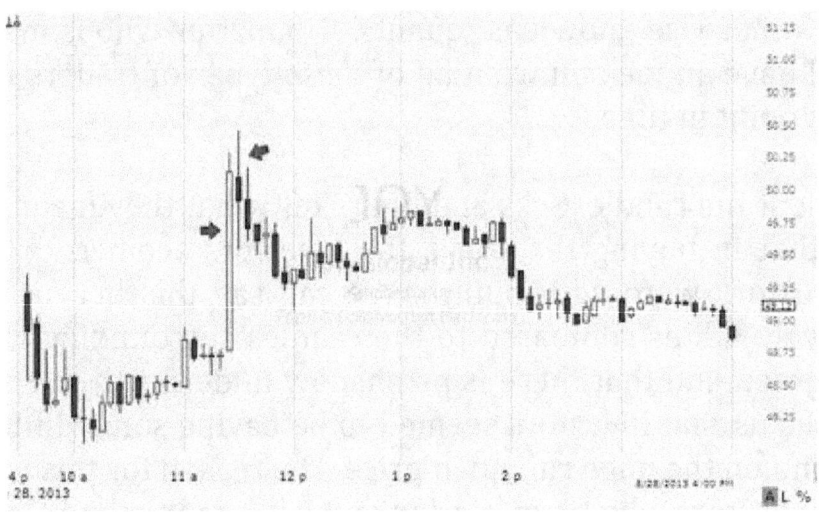

You would notice that in the above chart, the two candles show the high points for STEEL on that trading day. When the price was pulled back down and seemed to have resisted those new highs, such price would tend to continue dropping for the duration of the day. We can, therefore, say that candles can show us a story and that they can reveal to us some things about investor sentiment. Even when there is no poll or survey taken, and there's no interaction made with the other traders, we can simply listen to the story that these candles have and become better traders as a result.

Moving Averages

Since we are focusing on price movement, it should be noted that traders use a number of tools which are considered as derivatives of price. In short, traders employ several technical indicators that deliver various ways of analyzing the movement in price. The simplest among these is what we call "moving average." The latter actually comes in a number of flavors and the simplest among them is the one labeled as "simple moving average." Perhaps you have heard the media people talking about the Dow's 200-day moving average. Let's take a look at the math that is behind such concept. Say for example we take the closing price of the DJ-30 for the past trading days of 200. We then add them up and then divide by 200. The result gives us the Dow's 200 SMA (simple moving average).

Take note that other moving averages are also available and that such concept that uses a moving average can actually be used to a number of technical indicators apart from the price. Among the day traders, the most significant moving average is the one labeled as 20 EMA (exponential moving average). I don't intend to do the math involved in all of these several types of technical indicators. I just want to reiterate that an exponential moving average simply puts more emphasis on the more recent prices compared to the simple moving average which in turn gives equal weight to all prices. When we talk about 20 EMA, it's also important that we specify the time frame involved. For example, a 20 EMA of a 5-minute chart should be viewed differently from a 20 EMA of a chart that has a 60-minute time frame. The first one equates to having 100 minutes of data while the second would deliver data content of 1200 minutes. When we do day trading, our main focus will have to be on the smaller time frames. This means we can use twenty X 1-minute charts, twenty X 5-minute charts, etc.

Let's go back at the STEEL chart. Here, we try to add a 20 EMA to the 5-minute chart and then figure out how it looks.

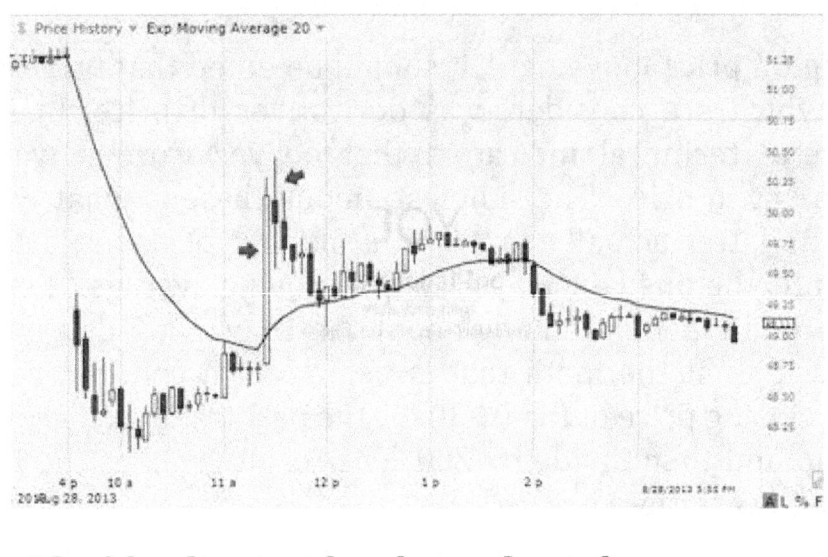

On the above chart, we can see the 20 EMA as shown by the blue line. The latter represents an exponential moving average of the past 20 5-minute candles. We call this a moving average because when each of the new 5-minute candle is seen added to the chart, it causes the earliest of the past 20 candles to fall out of the averaged formula while another candle is being added.

We may then ask ourselves why this is important and why we should be interested about the 20 EMA. At this point, I want to ask you a question. Looking at the chart, when do you think did we notice the higher spike of the big price? The answer is when the price moved above the 20 EMA. Do you think this is a coincidence? I don't think so. Remember that there some indicators that a number of traders use and that the 20 EMA is just one of them. It also acts like a self-filling prophecy. If everyone else thinks that the price crossing the 20 EMA on a chart with a 5-minute time frame is significant, there are two things that are bound to happen. First, traders would opt to buy the stock long since it has displayed evidence of price strength. Second, there are some traders who had fallen short on this stock that made them decide to buy the stock to cover their shorts. All these buying pressure, when occurring at the same time, causes more traders to plunge into the trade as they notice that the price is going up. Likewise, the price will continue to move up until that point when traders begin to claim their profit on the price run up and when there are fewer traders who are buying the stock long at such higher prices. The price would then go back to the EMA line, finds some support, and then fall back down later in the afternoon. In your opinion, do you think it's important that your charts have the 20 EMA? The answer must be yes.

We talked about "shorting stocks." Let me explain it further. Most people believe that it's possible to make money in trading stocks when they buy stocks long. In other words, you opt to buy a stock when the price is low, expecting that the price will continue to go higher so that you would be able to sell it and then earn some profit from that higher price. On the opposite side of this is what we refer to as "short selling." Allow me to explain this as simple as I can. Shorting a stock simply means that you are selling the stock at a high price along with the expectation that the price will drop at a lower rate, allowing you to "cover your short" (purchase the stock long in order to equal out the involved transaction) and earn some profit.

Normally, it takes traders some time to get themselves better acquainted with the idea of shorting stocks. Perhaps they think that they're making a mistake when they make money on a stock as the price becomes lower. However, this is what the game of trading is all about which means that you have the potential to make money in the market no matter if the stocks are moving up or moving down.

Let's say you shorted STEEL on that day prior to the time when it gapped down on the 28th. We say that you decided to short it at $51.25. Then when morning comes, the price falls down, and it hits $48.25. This only shows that if you decide to cover your shorts at the amount of $48.25, you are bound to earn a per share rate of $3 on doing such trade. If, for example, you shorted 500 shares, this will then cost you $25,625 with additional brokers fees (500 shares X $51.25 for every share. Let's use $10 as brokers fees to make it easier). If you covered those shorts using the price $48.25, the computation would be: 500 shares X $48.25 equals $24,125. We then deduct this from $25,625 to arrive at $1500. Then, we continue by deducting the $10 brokers fees. We would then arrive at $1490 which will be the profit. This shows that on this way of trading, you would make a profit of $1490.00.

Another way that we can analyze profits is through ROI (Return on Investment). What we should do here is we take the $1490 of net profit and then divide it by $25,625, the original amount. The ROI that we get as a result is 5.8 percent. The same 5.8 percent ROI can be achieved if we divide the per-share profit of $3 by the original price of $51.25.

We have included new terms such as "shorting" and "ROI" as they are essential terms to know for any day trader. We shall now go to back to our technical indicators and explore even further.

A number of traders employ multiple moving averages on their charts. As an example, let's add a 5 SMA to the STEEL chart. It should then look something like this:

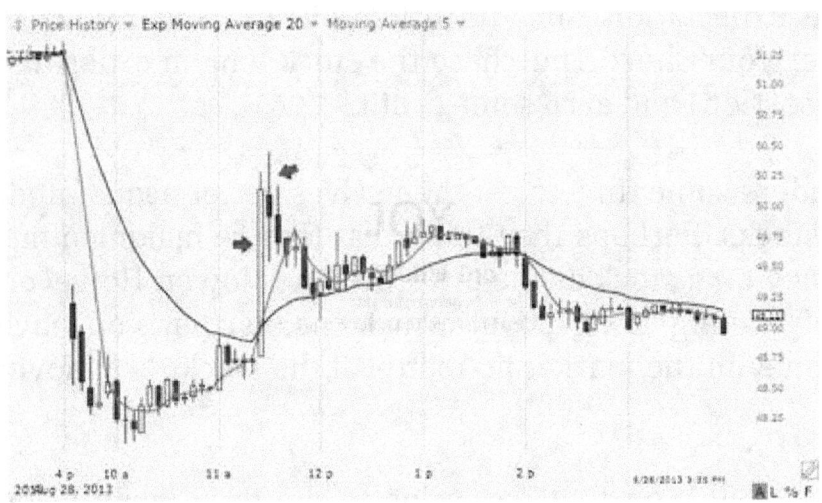

When you look at the chart above, do you notice a certain pattern?

Here, we can see the red line as the 5 SMA and that it crossed above the 20 EMA. This means that buyers of the stock pushed the price higher. If, for example, the same red line (5 SMA) crossed the 20 EMA but this time it's below, it means that sellers of the stock pushed the price lower. This gives us an example of what is referred to as a "moving average crossover." Here, there are two numbers that are normally used in order to create crossover patterns. When we begin to notice the pattern 011 in some varying charts, we can then describe this chart pattern as a high probability. Therefore, is it okay to assume that we could just trade this single pattern and then end up becoming rich? Most probably not. In reality, we should expect that all charts will not be as easy as what we think of them to be. Additionally, there is one critical information you need to know when you look at these charts: they are historical charts.

Historical charts are more like completed charts and not live charts. Notice that when the 5 SMA crosses right above the 20 EMA, it all seemed like it occurred simultaneously along with the big green candle. However, when you are trading the charts, and it's in real time, things may look differently. One of the moving averages' weaknesses is based on the fact that they lag price. You may then ask what I meant when I said that. If it is a moving average, we should then notice how the moving average would always lack the last price action as seen on the chart. If we are indeed looking at this as a 5-minute chart, we should clearly see how all of the upward price movement could have happened within the initial minute of the 5-minute candle. When the time comes that the 5 SMA crosses on top of the 20 EMA, the several upward movement may have already happened. I'm not talking like this to burst your bubble. I'm talking simply because it is true and that it is important for you to be aware of the strengths and the weaknesses of all technical indicators. With historical charts, you should remember that they do look differently than the live charts.

Some day traders use time frames that are smaller in order to try and catch the beginnings of such crossover events. As an example, let's use a 2-minute time frame and then leave those indicators at the same settings that were used before. Notice how our 20 EMA shall arrive at only minutes of data (20 candles X 2) while the 5-minute EMA have 100 minutes of data (20 candles X 5).

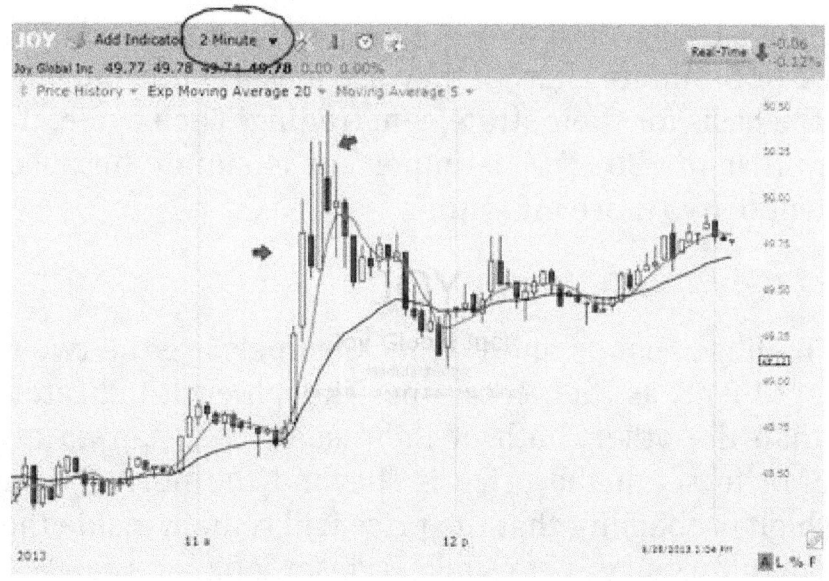

Here we want to stress on two things from the chart above. First, we can see that the 5 SMA crossed on top of the 20 EMA prior to the big price spike. This means that there's a chance we'd get into the trade earlier by using this smaller time frame. Second, when we solely use the moving average crossover as our point of reference in our trading strategy, we could find ourselves getting in and out of the trade a little too often as we can based from how we see the lines would intersect with each other for seven unique times within this 3-hour chart.

There are times when you may think that some indicators can be best used as a confirming indicator instead of as a predictive indicator. This is what I mean when I said such statement. If, by nature, the moving average crossover is a lagging indicator because it should wait for the price to move in order to show us direction, it would then be better for us not to wait on the actual crossover to happen before entering trade. We would probably have waited for a long time at this point. It could be better that we watch the price itself when it moves across the 20 EMA instead of waiting for the lagging 5 MA to give us the trade signal. However, the 5 MA crossover could be a good indicator for us to support our decision. When we see the moving average crossover after entering trade, it then makes us feel good that our trade decision was confirmed as a good one. When we don't see any confirmation, we might feel that we are on the alert because the decision we made could have been premature.

Again, let's try to go back to the 20 EMA. I mentioned earlier that it is used by a number of day traders. However, it may not be easy for us to find out if these traders use it on a 2 or 5-minute chart, if they use it as a confirming indicator, or if they use it as the basis for their strategy in trading. Then again, the other reason why we say that the 20 EMA is important is simply because it is a significant component of two more indicators.

Bollinger Bands and Keltner Channels

Indicators such as Bollinger Bands and Keltner Channels are the two popular ones which use the 20 EMA as their focal line. Though each indicator uses a different formula than the other, both of them seek to assign an area that surround the 20 EMA to see if the price is "beyond the norm." Using both systems gives us a high probability that the price will remain inside the bands that are created by their formulas. Let us take a closer look.

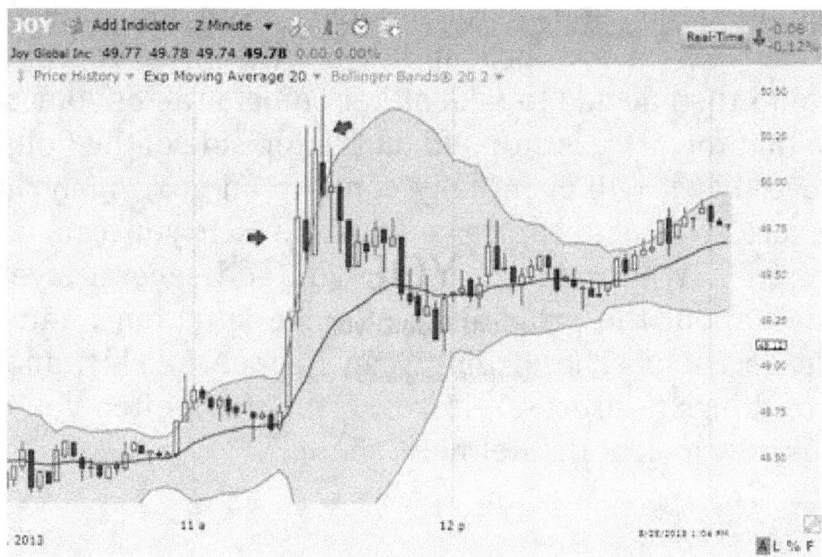

By staying with our 2-minute chart, eliminating the red line that represents the 5 SMA, and adding the Bollinger Bands' standard setting, we can arrive at the results shown in the chart above. There are two things we can say about this chart that are in line with high probability trading. First, take note that when the price crosses on top of the 20 EMA, it has the tendency to remain in the Bollinger Band's upper channel. Second, see how the price candles remain outside the Bollinger Bands within a small amount of time.

On the huge price run up that took place between the two blue arrows, we notice that the price candles are running along the upper part of the Bollinger Bands. However, for the remaining period of time, the price is fairly well contained inside those bands.

Let us now start to add things up. Using your knowledge about this stock (it is what we call as a gap down stock which is caused by a bad earnings report) along with your knowledge of candle structure (the price looked as if it was pushed back down following a quick run up in price) and your knowledge of Bollinger Bands (the price shows it has the tendency to stay inside the bands), do you think that the price would highly likely continue to run higher and remain on top of the Bollinger bands? The answer is most probably not.

Do you understand at this point what you just did? You have actually combined several elements of technical analysis which is significant in making a high probability trading decision. Using this knowledge, if you had been on this trade long while the price was moving up, you might find this information handy to temper your greed and gather some profit on the trade. Understanding that there was a low probability for the price to continue getting higher, you would then decide to take either some or all of your profit as long as you still see that the price is situated on the top side of the Bollinger Bands since you believe that it will eventually come to an end. Analyzing in this manner is the exact type of technical analysis which you can use to become a profitable trader. What you do is that you add several layers of technical analysis, think about the probability of some situations, and then coming up with trade decisions. These things can happen quickly, and our mind may have a lot of things to process. However, the more often you do it, the easier it gets. Let us now look at the Keltner Channels.

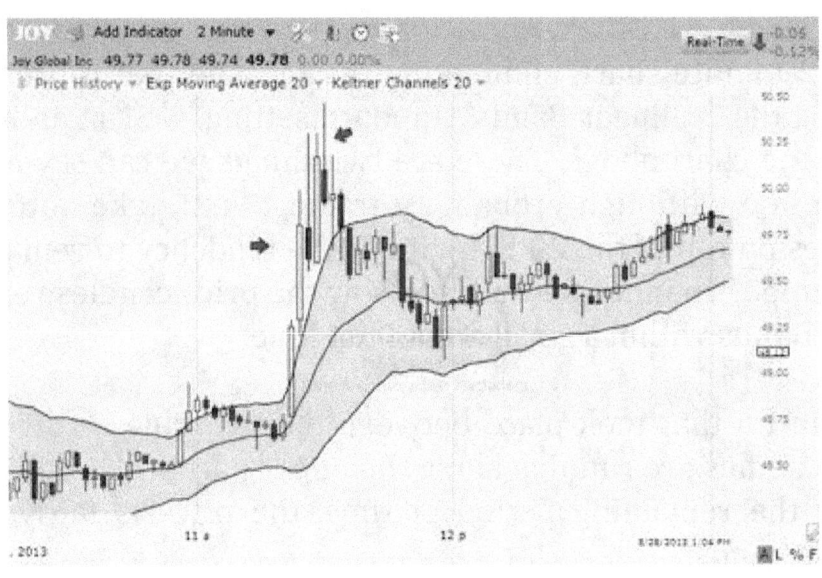

In the above chart, we can see that the Bollinger Bands has been removed and that the Keltner Channel has been added. We can also see that the chart shows some added contrast to the candles that ran up quickly. They appear to be sticking far above the top of the Kelther Channel in order for the trader to understand their abnormal behavior.

There are some traders who use the Bollinger Bands (thought to be the most popular) while some use the Keltner Channels. Other traders even use both. However one chooses, it is still important to have these on your charts for you to see what the other traders are considering into and also to give you some help in executing your high probability strategies.

Strength Indicators

Going back to the last group of technical indicators, we can say that those bands which surrounded the 20 EMA help us to see the prices that were "outside the norm" or those prices that are outside the price's normal range. By this, we can identify if a stock could be subjected to a possible price pull back. However, there are other indicators used by day traders which help them to come up with this analysis. Some of these indicators are what we refer to as oscillators since they tend to deviate on a scale of zero to 100. Again, we should take note that these technical indicators are derived from the price.

Another type of oscillator is what we call as Relative Strength Index (RSI). Based on the name, this oscillator type is used to find the stock's strength relative to the present price trend. While it does have the range of zero to 100, there are certain lines that are being closely watched by traders. Remember, if we notice that other traders are taking a closer look at certain lines and indicators, then we should also be looking at such.

Let's look at the chart of STEEL.

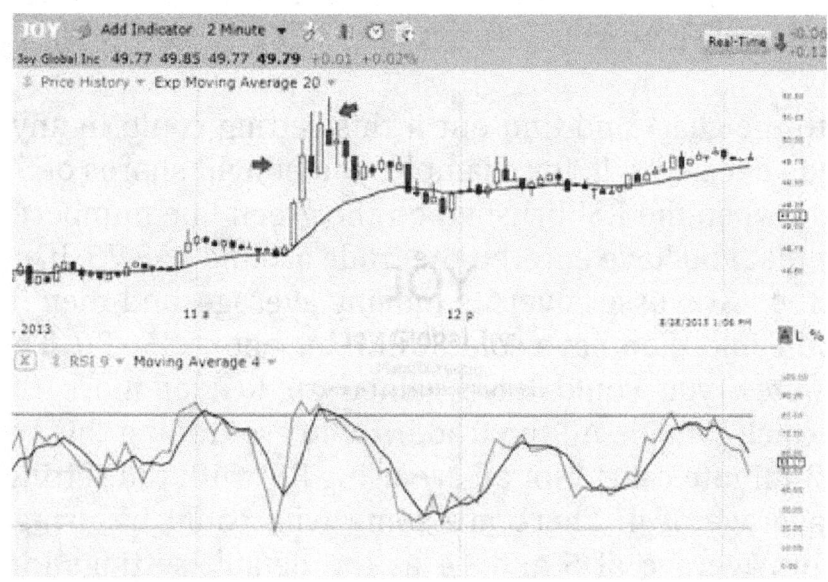

If you notice, the chart is the familiar 2-minute chart that we were looking at earlier and that it still shows the price spike that happened on the morning of August 28, 2013. At this point, we didn't include the Bollinger Bands and Keltner Channels to allow us to focus on this new indicator. Notice how the

RSI indicator is placed in a separate pane below the price. Notice also how two horizontal lines were added to the RSI pane. A red line is drawn at $0 while a green one is drawn at 20. Moreover, you can see that the RSI is placed with the number 9 beside and that the moving average is set at 4. At this point, we shall explain all of these numbers.

Note that the RSI's standard horizontal line settings are 70 and 30 and not 80 and 20. This is the reason we have stretched the areas out a little. The general idea tells us that when RSI seemed greater than 80, it means that the stock is overbought and can be subjected to a price pullback. On the other hand, when the RSI is smaller than 20, it means that the stock is oversold and can be subjected to a bounce. Let's not get into the technical detail for RSI and talk about the mathematical formula since doing so could make us feel overwhelmed with so much detail at this point. It is crucial that we know what the indicator is meant to measure, we know how other traders view it, and we also know how these traders use it.

Also, notice how I've also changed another part of the RSI on the chart above. We can see that the default setting for RSI was changed from 14 to 9. I made the change so as to make the indicator a bit more sensitive to price since we are using such for day trading. Moreover, I have adjusted the moving average of RSI on this chart and made it as 4.

Let us now go back to the chart and find out if this setting could in any way help us in making trade decisions. If, for example, you bought shares of STEEL long at about 11:15AM when the RSI brushed on the green line numbered 20, it is then highly likely that you have entered the trade around $48.75. If, on the other hand, you saw the RSI crosses over its moving average, and then it falls below the 80 line, you could then have sold STEEL for about $50.00. Then in less than fifteen minutes, you could have gained an ROI of more than 2 percent! There's one catch though. All the traders who are trading this type of stock do not use the 2-minute chart. Not all are using RSI with the setting of 9 and with a moving average of 4. There are some who could be using a 5-minute chart, a moving average of 5 and 14 as the default settings for RSI. Moreover, they could be using the standard 70 and 30 settings for overbought and oversold.

Let us now see how the chart would like after we have changed all of the settings.

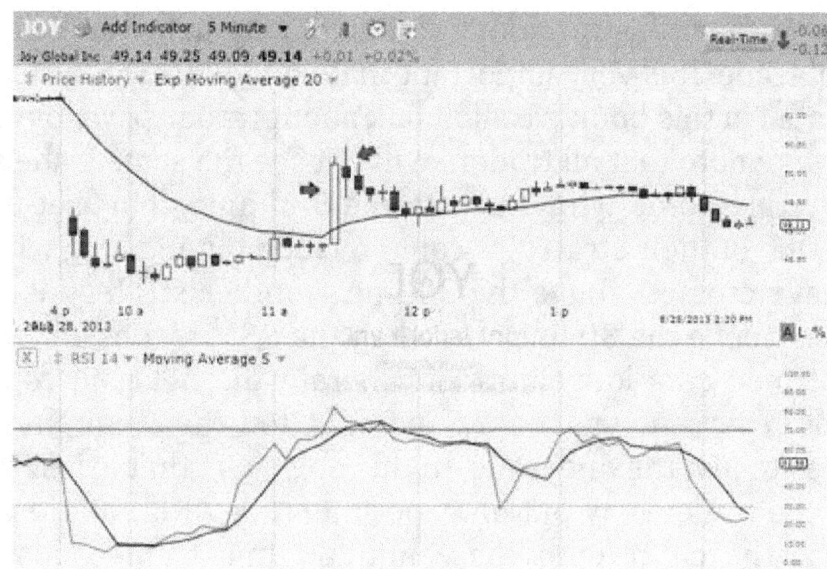

Based on the chart above, notice how changing the time frame would give us a significantly different view of what is going on with the stock. By changing the settings, we get an absolutely different read on when it's best to enter and to exit this type of trade. Which setting is, therefore, correct?

There is no single perfect method for technical analysis. While it is true that some of the indicators could be set using their default settings such as Bollinger Bands, it is also fairly okay to play with the settings found on other indicators. There are, however, a few key points here that should not be overlooked.

First, there is no such thing as "one perfect system" when trading stocks. A lot of new traders believe that all they have to do is conduct several testing and tweaking until they discover the perfect set-up. Once this is achieved, it is then assumed that one will get every trade with no mistake, and that money should never be an issue again. This needs a wakeup call! The truth is, there is no single way to trade. There is no single system that fits all users. One example is when there are traders who would prefer to use the 5-minute or 10-minute charts when they do day trading. Some of these traders never go higher than the 1-minute chart. You need to discover what it is that works best for you. The only way to know about it is by experimenting with a number of settings using various indicators and time frames until a set-up which works for you is reached.

Second, note that both chart set-ups above could actually help you gain some profit on this type of trade. It is very important that you follow the system that you have created. Later in this book we shall talk about trader psychology. For now, however, just take note that all traders will not see the same trade and at the same time. There are some who may use the 5-minute chart set-up that was just displayed. One of their strategies could include buying long when the RSI 14 is seen to have crossed above the 30 line. Another strategy is selling when the RSI 14 goes above the 30 line and when the RSI 14 goes underneath the 70 line. It is deemed as a longer trader wherein the net gain could fall somewhere around 2 percent vs. the 2.5 percent for the 2-minute chart. However, this applies to just the one trade on this one chart that is just for this single day. In time, the trader may opt on experimenting with both ideas and later on decide that the chart with the 3-minute time frame and having different RSI settings has the highest success probability of 7 for the certain type of stocks that they are trading. In other words, there is no single way to do the trade.

There is no such thing as a single perfect set-up for your charts. You should be able to experiment and find out what it is that works best for you. Then again, let's continue and discuss another popular oscillator.

A technical indicator, the Stochastic Oscillator also oscillates between zero and 100 and measures overbought and oversold areas on the chart. Let's take a look on how it is on our STEEL chart.

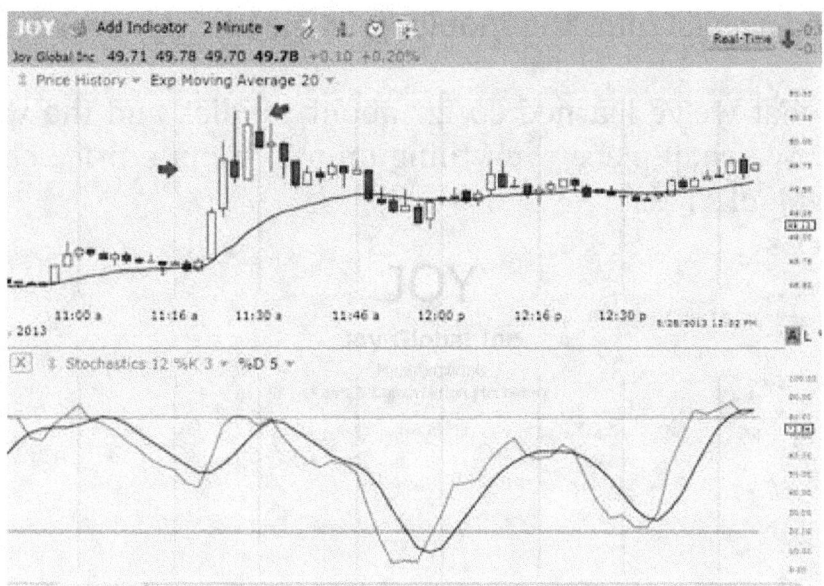

Note that the default settings for Stochastics are used in the chart although it also shows that the 80 and 20 lines have been added. When you take a look at the chart above, do you notice anything?

On the whole, we note that price tends to drop lower every time the red line goes beyond 80. Likewise, the price seems to bounce every time the red line drops below 20. You should remember that an oscillator is not supposed to go lower than zero or higher than 100. This means that hitting those lines does not connote of an immediate rise or fall of the price at those lines. It does not show what the indicator wants to tell you. What it does say is "in line with the previous 14 candles, the price is either high or low." Likewise, it's not the same as saying that the price is expected to turn around at this point. Note that the RSI and the Stochastic can stay beyond and even below on both 80 and 20 lines for prolonged periods of time when there's a strong trending occurrence of a stock. That is, in reality, a mistake that a number of new traders make.

These traders would say "Well, the Stochastic Oscillator shows that the stock is overbought." What they do next is to short the stock based only on this notion. Then again, the reading stays above $0 while the stock continues trending higher and the new trader continues holding onto his short sell of the stock as he waits for the price to drop. Meanwhile, the Stochastic stays on top of the $0 and then the trader seems to continue losing more and more money with the trade moving against him. You should not make the same mistake!

Let's put together what we've learned so far about candles and the various technical indicators. We shall place everything on a 2- minute price chart of STEEL and see how it looks like.

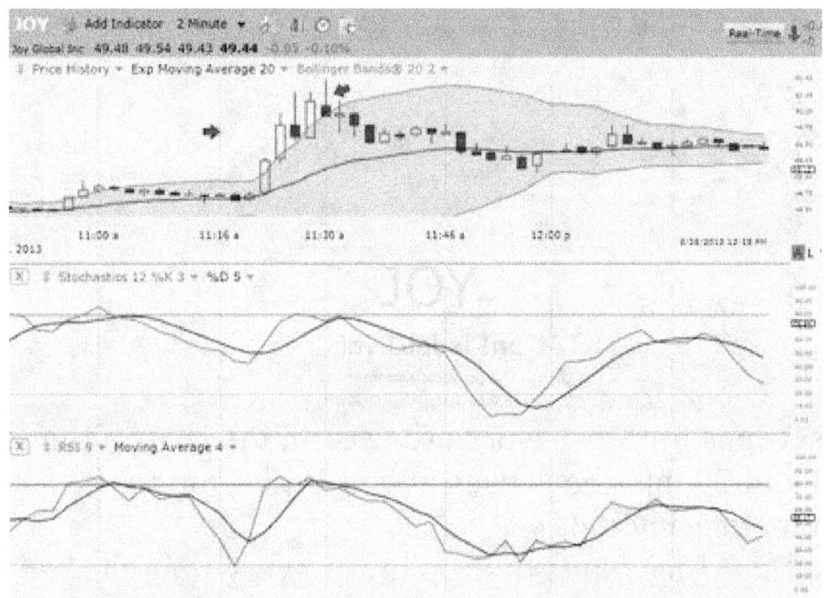

Judging from what you've learned so far, notice any high probability long trade on the chart above? Do you think you can write down those ideas and see if you can apply them on the other charts? I'm sure you can. Let's just go ahead and list everything down here.

Rule 1. Buy long when all of the following conditions are met in the chart:

a. The price is above the 20 EMA;

b. The Stochastics red line (12 percent K 3) crosses beyond the blue line (%D 5); and

c. The RSI 9 crosses beyond its 4 MA.

Rule 2. Sell when any two of the following conditions are seen on the chart:

a. The price seemed to be re-entering the inside part of the Bollinger band top line;

b. The Stochastic red line is seen crossing back down beneath the blue line;

c. The RSI is seen crossing back down beneath its 4 MA.

What we did here is we have just created a trading strategy! But don't treat it like any old trading strategy. We can treat it as a high probability trading strategy if the following statements are true:

1. It is based on the objective criteria derived from technical analysis of our charts;

2. It has a definite criteria set for entering the trade;

3. It has a definite criteria set for exiting the trade;

4. We are done with back testing the idea on a definite group of stocks and learned that there is a high probability of success;

5. As time moves on, we learned that trading this strategy in real time would lead to earning a profit.

These final two points are still unclear at this point. We were able to look at just a single stock in a day. We need to have a larger sampling of trades in order to find out if this is really a high probability strategy. Just like what I've mentioned earlier, we need to determine if using such strategy will actually work in real time on live charts. When we look back at indicator crossovers and historical charts, it is easy to believe that we have found the perfect strategy.

But then again, it is in paper trading such strategy over several charts that we learned about whether it is a high probability trading strategy or it is not.

After we have tested such strategy, we may learn that this strategy actually works better with certain stocks than the others. Suppose that the stock we want to examine (STEEL) was a gap down stock on that day when the market seemed to be trending higher. We may need to add that factor to our list of criteria when entering the trade. We may learn that there are other criteria that should be added. For example, STEEL normally trades with more than 2 million shares traded for every day. If we would try to use this strategy on a stock that trades at only 200,000 shares each day, we may understand that the strategy's probability of success is less.

When we look at the share price, we may find that those stocks which are under $10 for every share would not work as well using this strategy. If, for example, we combine low share price along with low volume, we may find that in reality, it does loses money! This only means that we need to consider some variables before we can move up and down and think that we've already found the perfect high probability trading strategy.

At this point, you could be thinking, "It's only now that we realized a lot of things are involved in trading stocks." This feeling is common among traders who are new in the field. However in your case, the difference is that you are beginning to realize some of those variables that are needed to make a winning strategy. Being a new trader, you are learning how to avoid some of those common mistakes. You are learning that when it comes to good trading, there should be a high probability trading strategy which has been back tested in real time; that there are specific rules when entering and exiting the trade; and that could work best according to some of the present market conditions. So, congratulations because at this point, you have already learned a lot.

Before we finally leave this section, we would like to mention one more technical indicator. The Moving Average Convergence Divergence (MACD) is another type of popular indicator that some traders use which deserves our attention here.

Let's probe further by using our chart of STEEL:

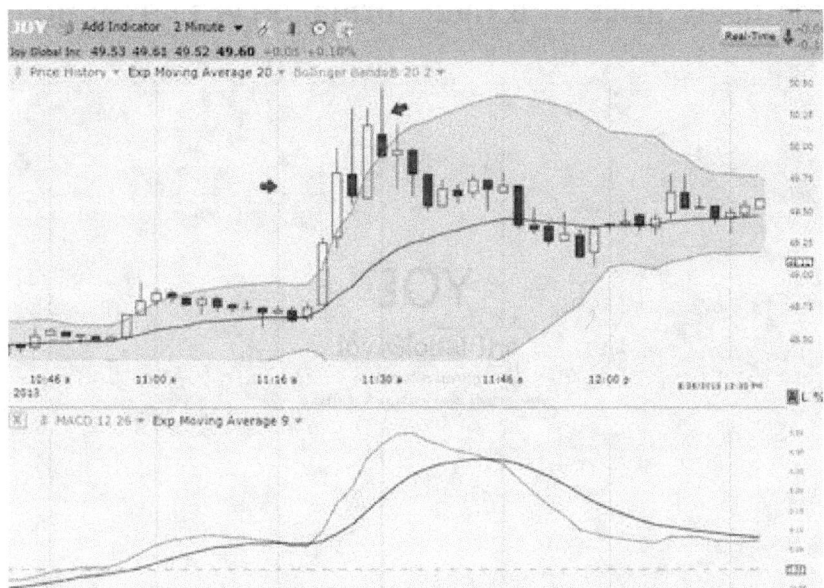

Take note that the MACD indicator is composed of several moving averages. Note that in the chart above, I'm using the standard setting of MACD wherein we get a 12 26 setting and 9 as our exponential moving average. You will also notice the dashed line found at the bottom of the chart at zero. The dashed line is what we call the signal line. The term "convergence divergence" refers to the two lines found on the chart. When the lines move further apart, it means they "diverge." When the price begins to drop lower, the moving averages "converge" and will continue to do so until they cross down and then they would diverge again.

Let's now put more focus on the MACD. If, for example, the MACD is found above the signal line where it crosses above the 9 EMA, we may consider this a bullish signal. If you considered this as your indicator, you could then go long when you find that signal on the chart. We can consider a wide divergence as an extreme stretching of price. Likewise, the flattening of the light blue line indicates that such lines could begin to converge again which we should think as a possible warning that we take profit on the trade. If we see a MACD cross down pattern with both lines seen below the signal line, we should consider this as a possible short set up.

So far, all of the technical indicators that I've already mentioned are derivatives of price. There is one indicator that is not that strictly based on price and this is volume. A number of volume indicators are actually available with some of them even using price into their formula. Let us then look at volume in the next chart.

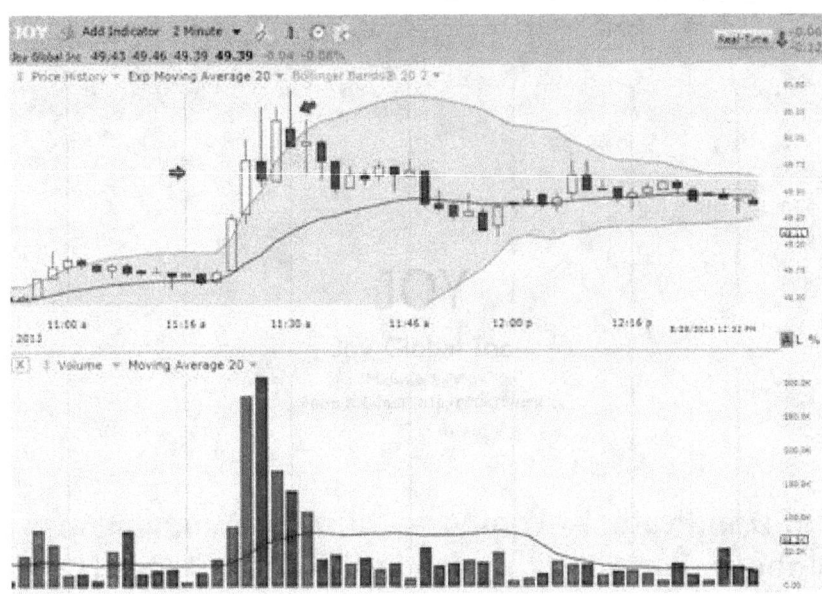

Looking at the volume pane's far right, you can see the number of traded shares. Notice how the volume bars spike at the rally point that we've been studying. The green and red colors tell us whether the buyers or the sellers are once again dominating the price. In the end, the volume will fall back lower than its 20 MA which we can also see being plotted on the pane.

Try to imagine about hundreds of various indicators. Just like what I've said before, most of these indicators are variations on a theme which makes us ask "what is the price doing?" Remember that trading entails a lot of decision making and for this, we use the technical indicators as a way to help us arrive at a final decision. We also need to watch these technical indicators since other traders also use them when they are trading.

Not a single perfect indicator will ever be enough to do the job for you. It is then important that you experiment with several indicators and find those which you feel comfortable with in using and those which give you the best signals. A piece of caution: never overdo the indicators. There are some traders who think that "the more is better" which is a mistake and is absolutely not true. The problem lies in the fact that you add a lot of indicators but as you add, you stop looking at the price. Several charts of traders that I've seen so far would show lines, indicators, and moving averages except the price candles. Note therefore that price is a primary component. Almost every indicator relies on price movement that is something that you need to watch. However, since your chart has too many indicators, you may suffer from the so-called "information overload." Too much information will cause you to get confused which later on could result to inaction. You can be compared to a deer that cannot move when he's caught in the headlights. You should then be able to create a chart layout that has more clarity. Never get it cluttered with so many indicators. You should be able to learn what works best for you and then you can start to feel comfortable with it. Avoid constantly adding and subtracting indicators and changing the settings in search for the perfect one as doing so will make you feel confuses. What you need to do is find just a few indicators that you like and then use them every day. By doing so, you get an idea of their strengths and weaknesses. Moreover, you would feel more and more comfortable with them as time goes by.

Chapter 5: Analyzing List of Stocks

In the Tape Reader, though the person is determined to operate exclusively using one stock, he should keep his eyes open to what is happening to the other people around him. There are a number of opportunities that can come up from anywhere. As a way to prove this, let's look at the market in the early fall of 1907. During this period, Union Pacific was in the lead after rising from below 150 to 167 5/8. Within a span of three or four days prior to the culmination of its advancement, there was heavy selling observed in Smelters, Steel, Copper, St. Paul and Reading, which are all under the scope of the Union's strength.

There's no doubt that this became the market's turning point. One needs to just go short of Reading and then wait for the break. He could also have played Union on a close stop under the belief that there will be a collapse in the whole market right after the Union turned downward. A number of things can occur once the stock liquidation was accomplished. These include the halt in Union's advancing, withdrawal of the supporting orders, and the occurrence of the "pre-election break." This totaled to more than a 20 point decline in Union while the rest of the groups list went on proportionate declines.

The operator who has his eyes fixed solely on Union may have been surprised with all these; if only he had seen the whole market, he could have known what is about to occur. By simply determining the point of distribution, he could take a closer look on the accumulation that should come next. He could also be aware of the level where there is an expected support at the very least. If only he had the expertise to trace this, he could have made some quick money as well.

While it is true that there are some stocks that make up the backbone or the leadership position, this significant member forms only a single part of the market body which is very similar to the physical structure of a human being. Let's say that Union Pacific is strong and that it is advancing. Out of a sudden, New York Central had a weakness attack; Consolidated Gas went on a decline; American Ice was nauseous and weak; Great Western and Southern Railway suffered just the same. Perhaps there is absolutely nothing wrong with the "leader." However, its strength will be compromised by the others' weaknesses.

The Brooklyn Rapid Transit may be hit with a bad break which is caused by a political attack or any other local influence. It's impossible for it to have an effect on the business of the huge transportation stocks, otherwise called trans continentals. Still, Union, St. Paul and Reading went on a decline by as much as the B.R.T. We can say that a person who had his finger suddenly crushed may pass out as a result of the shock to his nervous system. However, the member who had an injury will have no effect to the other members or other functions of the body.

The chain on the time-worn illustration which is as strong as its weakest link will not serve. When such weak link breaks, it causes the chain to break into two parts, with each of the part having the same strength as its weakest link. The same thing goes with the market. It does not break in two no matter how severe the blow it receives.

Note that a huge break could occur when something unexpected comes along. This could be in the form of a financial disaster, a rise in the interest rates, a drop in investment demand, a battered public sentiment or confidence; or a deeply affected corporate earning power which can also appear as declining. But while there may be a sense of panic in the air, there is usually a level where the buying power earns some considerable strength that allows it to produce a rally or even a permanent upturn.

The Tape Reader should aim to operate in that stock where the widest swings and the broadest market are combined. Perhaps he may regard switching temporarily into other stocks as something to his advantage since this appears to deliver the fastest and the surest profits. So, it is important that we are familiar with the characteristics found in the principal speculative methods in order for us to judge their advantages at this point and also to realize their weight and bearing on any given market situation.

Another thing that you ought to know is that the market is created by the minds of not just one but a number of men. Whatever state of mind these men have, it is reflected in the securities prices where their owners operate. Let us probe further some of these individuals and the influences behind some stocks and some groups of stocks as seen in a number of relationships. Doing so will allow us to determine their respective power and how such will affect everything on the list or a particular issue that we choose to operate.

Let us now identify the market leaders at this point for illustration purposes. We have Smelters, Anaconda, St. Paul, Reading and Union Pacific. Professionals, manipulators and the general public get most of their inspiration from the moves of these six issues which saw a concentration of forty to eighty percent of the total daily transactions except during the "war" markets that took place between 1914 and 1916. We shall then refer to them as the "Big Six." As a Tape Reader, one should be able to understand the basic principles underlying the market. This includes the principle that leadership changes frequently. But for the sake of our own purpose, we need to concentrate on this list.

Out of the Big Six on our list, three of them are mainly influenced by the buying and selling movement of a group that is known as the Kuhn-Loeb-Standard Oil. They have four stocks namely Anaconda, Reading, St. Paul, and Union. Smelters is then handled by the Guggenheims while Steel, which is under the control of Morgan, is without a doubt had been shaken up and down which was caused by public sentiment more than anything else.

Naturally, the state of the steel trade is the integral component of all the important movements in this trading issue. Occasionally, Morgan or any other with a large interest may decide to buy or sell a few hundred shares. In general, however, it is the public's attitude which mainly affects the price of the Steel a common notion. Perhaps this is something that should stay strictly in the mind since it makes a useful guide to the market's technical position, allowing the market's overbought or oversold condition to be turned on.

Let us now take a look at the term "Secondary Leaders" which comes next in importance. We can compare this term to something which, at times, burst into a huge activity while being accompanied by large volume. They are called "Secondary Leaders" because even though they rarely influence the Big Six to a certain extent, the less significant issues are usually found within their initiative.

Another group is what we shall call as the "Minor Stocks" which is made up of less important issues with most of them low-priced and has a number of public favorites.
There are some who, upon seeing an advance done in some of the Minor stocks, decide to buy the Primary or Secondary Leaders, under the condition that the latter will be affected on a bullish level. While this could occur at

times, most of the time, it doesn't. It is then a mistake to expect a 5,000 share trader to follow the patterns in trading of a 100 share trader, or a man with 100 shares to be influenced into buying and selling of the trader with 10 shares.

We can compare the number of stocks in the market to that of a huge fleet of boats wherein each are being hitched with one another and being towed by the tugs which we would call as "Business Conditions" and "Interest Rate." Note that in the first row, we have the Big Six while behind them, we have the Minors, the Secondary Leaders, and the Miscellaneous issues. Remember that generating steam and having the fleet under way will need some time. The same goes true for the leaders. They are the first to feel the impulse while the others in turn would follow.

If, by the chance, the tugs are placed on a halt, the fleet will continue to move for a while with its own momentum. This can occur with some level of bumping, hacking and filling.

If in case there is an abrupt change in the tugs' direction, the bumping can become severe. Naturally, those who are on the rear will not be able to earn a leadership role unless they do an all-around readjustment.

The Leaders that we are referring to are representative of the greatest industries in the U.S. These include mining, steel making, and railroading. Naturally, these stocks should be treated as the main outlet for the country's speculative actions. The St. Paul and Union Pacific systems are in charge of the entire West. Reading, which is by itself a huge railroad property, is the dominant figure in the coal mining industry. It is very much interlaced with the other railroads which only goes to show the typical Eastern scenario. Steel, on its part, is tightly bound up with the side of the general business across the nation while Smelters and Anaconda are the manipulating factors in the smelting industry and copper mining.

This is the right way of looking at groups of stocks. Who is the group's Primary Leader? Who should be considered as the Secondary Leaders and who should be the Minor issues?

When we are able to classify the principal active stocks, we can see more clearly what are those forces that make them move. For example, when we see that Consolidated Gas suddenly gains strength and increases in activity, we can say that it will highly likely affect Brooklyn Union Gas. However, we don't see any reason other stocks should advance further and should do so out of sympathy.

Then, when we see that all the stocks that belong in the Standard Oil group moves a step further in a way that is steady and constant, it only shows that the capitalists involved have immersed themselvess in a bull campaign. Considering that these people never enter deals for a few points, it may be safe to ride along with them for a short while, at least until distribution seemed apparent.

The outbreak of speculation occurring in Colorado Fuel does not actually become a bull argument on the other stocks of Steel. If, for example, it was based on the conditions of trade, U.S. Steel would definitely be the first one to feel the impetus which would then reflect on the others.

When we select the best stock from the Kuhn-Loeb-Standard Oil group, the Tape Reader should consider whether the conditions surrounding the situation are agreeable to the greatest activity and volumes in the railroad or in the industrial stocks. Considering the former case, the choice would either be St. Paul or Union Pacific. The latter case would then be Anaconda. Erie may then be able to come out of its rut (similar to how it was in the summer of 1907 when its selling price was at around 24), and assume leadership in the low-priced stocks. Apparently, this shows some important development in Erie while a rise in every low-priced stocks is not foreshadowed.

If, however, a strong rise begins in the Union Pacific, then it continues with the Southern Pacific while others in the group also followed, the Tape Reader will then decide to get the leader and then stay with it. There's no way that he would waste his time on Erie since when it was moving up by 5 points, it could be assumed that Union Pacific may advance by 10 or 15 points, as long as doing so is a genuine move. A number of valuable deductions could be made after studying stocks groupings.

Experience tells us that when a Secondary Leader begins to rise, the Leaders are almost through in their advance and that distribution is already taking place which is then covered under the protection of the strength found in the

Secondary stock and even others that are in its class. Those who are trading professionally used to refer to this as stock indicators.

Having no inside manipulation in a stock allows operation of the pools. A number of the moves that are seen among these groups came from floor or office operators. They have successfully pushed their stock towards a desired direction by simply joining hands and using huge quantities of stock.

Let's say U.S. Steel is being swayed by certain conditions present in the steel trade along with the general public's speculative temper and occasional assistance coming from a few insiders. There's no other stock on the list that represents the true index of the public attitude nor the market's technical position. These include those who are out-right owners of the stock and those who bring it by the margin. Steel trade reports are scrutinized very carefully while the corporation's earnings and on hand orders are studied by thousands.

While the great public sells its favorite short only on rare occasions, it does carry it on margin until it has secured a profit or until it has become shaken with a rough decline. This means that if the stock is strong based on adverse news, we can say that public holdings must be strongly fortified and say so with a strong confidence. If for instance Steel displays greater weakness, we can therefore see an untenable position of the public.

Here, we would note that public sentiment appeared to be strongly bullish and that it has spread itself across the low-priced speculative shares. Junior steel stocks insiders become aware of this and would then decide to take advantage of it. They are able to move on and find a fairly good market that is meant for their holdings.

The stocks' chief inspiration is found in the orders for locomotives, cars, etc. which are placed by the railroads. Such orders are said to be dependent upon the business conditions in general. As a result, one should not expect much for the equipment issues to go beyond following the trend of prosperity or depression.

We should be able to introduce ourselves to the so-called principal speculative mediums as well as their families. As acquaintance become closer, we would then see how each seemed to bear a certain personality type. Finding ourselves in a room filled with as many as fifty or even a

hundred people who are all familiar to us according to their characteristics and chief motives, we are able to form concrete ideas regarding their probable actions based on a given set of circumstances.

It then behooves the Tape Reader to get himself familiar with even the slightest details relating to such market identities. The same goes with the habits, motives, and methods of the men who do the main moves on the Stock Exchange chess board.

Chapter 6: Rules in Trading

For a person who thinks about an extensive trip, the usual thing that is first taken into account is how much he would be spending on such. When we plan our excursion into the trading resort, we should be able to carefully weigh the impending expenses or even the fixed charges incurred in trading.

Should there be no expenses, it is then so much easier to make a profit. Here, profits would simply exceed that of losses. No matter if you're a member or not of the New York Stock Exchange, when doing actual trading – take note that profits must go ahead than losses and expenses. These are usually incurred in every trading activity regardless of whether there is a gain or loss.

They are made up of:
- Commissions
- "Invisible eighth" (the difference between the bid price and the asked price under the assumption that you are using the market price in buying and in selling)
- Sale's Income Tax
- Exchange fees

We can also add "interest" to the list if, for example, the trade has been carried over night.

If we purchase a New York Stock Exchange seat, we can then reduce the commission into $1 for every hundred shares if it is bought and sold within a single day. Otherwise, it reaches $3.12 if it is done over night. This can be offset in part by interest on assessments, dues, the seat cost, etc. Note that the "invisible eighth" is one type of factor that cannot be overcome by anyone even one is a member. Both the bid and the asked price can never be lower than an eighth apart. If the market is 45 ¼ to 3/8 during that time when you are buying, you should, as a rule, pay 45 3/8. This would become 45 V4 should you decide to sell it. Such hypothetical difference goes the same all through the trading process and has been referred to as the "invisible eighth" by the writer.

Knowing that the Tape Reader is not a member of the exchange, he should then realize that on that moment he initiates an order to go long or short 100 shares, he already lost an eighth of a point. To avoid fooling himself, he should consider adding his commissions to his purchase price. He could also immediately deduct such commission from his selling price.

Those who would usually boast of their profits normally would forget to deduct the expenses. But this is the significant item that usually places the net result over to the debit side.

We often hear the expression, "I got out even, but not for the commissions." Here, the speaker seemed to scorning what it appears like a trifling consideration. This type of self-deception can be destructive which can be seen when we compute the fixed charges on a 100 shares trade.

Always remember that a losing the commission on the first trade causes the amount to double on the second trade prior to securing a dollar of profit.

Therefore, we can say that the Tape Reader's problem is not just to eliminate losses but also to cover his expenses as soon as possible. Since there are some points profit in a long trade, he should be able to prevent the stock to run back below his net buying price.

The circumstances, in this case, appear to need a stop order which will disable him to be obliged in paying out money whatever happens. Such stop order should never be utilized if the net cost is very close to the market price. There must be a small reaction allowed.

By essence, a Tape Reader is the one who follows the immediate trend. An expert knows how to easily distinguish between a trend change and a reaction that is simple and minor.

A person's mental barometer has the ability to spot a change. When it indicates one, the person will never wait for a stop order to be caught. Rather instantly, he would clean his house or reverse his position. Therefore, we can say that the stop order should be treated as an advantage only during reversal cases as these are sudden and pronounced.

Another reason a stop should be placed is when the operator has the duty to leave the tape longer than a moment or if, without warning, the ticker suddenly went out of order. Though it may be true that he has his focus on the tape, it is the market that will tell him what he is supposed to do. Once this condition does not occur, he should act accordingly if he temporarily loses a sense of direction. He should be able to protect himself from such forces that are lurking in the dark which can attack him without any warning.

Let me cite a trader who, after buying 500 shares of Sugar, went out to have lunch. His bill cost 25 cents. Upon returning to the tape, he learned that his total bill has reached $5,000 and 25 cents! There was no stop order left. Sugar dropped up to ten points. The trader received a margin call from his broker.

Note that the ticker has this habit on being incoherent and usually, it shows up at the most critical points. Like a bad joke, it goes back to printing intelligibly only when the trouble has been solved and not prior to its occurrence. Since the loss of a quotation, even if there's only a few of them, should be deemed important, we should make sure that a stop is placed at once and allow it to stay until at least the flow of prices goes back to normal.

If, for example, a trade has to be performed over night, we have to make sure that a stop is entered after assuming that an accident to the trader or the market is possible. There could be an important event that may occur prior to the next day's opening which could have a violent effect on the stock. Perhaps the trader will have an illness, arrive late, or he can become incapacitated. We should always give an allowance to every kind of accidents.

Knowing where to place a stop under such conditions would depend on certain circumstances. Shrewd and experienced traders have the consensus which is agreeable to a maximum gross loss of two points on any single trade. This is in fact purely arbitrary. As a rule, the Tape Reader knows what he has to do whenever he is at the tape. However, any contingency that would make him separated from the market would require him to fall back upon the arbitrary stop.

Getting a closer stop is possible by simply noting the "points of resistance" in a stock. These are the levels at which we can see a turn in the market as a result of a reaction.

Let's cite an example. Assuming that you are short at 130, then the stock breaks up to 128. It rallies to 129 and then turns back down again. The point of resistance is measured at 129. Note that the more often it turns at 129, the stronger is your case.

In other cases where the service is temporarily absent or interrupted, a good stop is determined as 129V4 or 129 ¼. Otherwise known as "points of resistance," this shall be discussed in fuller detail later.

If, for example, the operator wants to use an automatic stop, there is a very good method to use in this type of situation.

Let's say the initial trade is composed of a one-point stop. With every ¼ pt, note that the stock moves according to your favor. You should, therefore, change the stop in order to correspond. This will enable the stop to be never more nor even less than a single point away from the extreme market price. Doing so will gradually and automatically reduce the risk. Moreover, if the

Tape Reader has the needed skills, he should expect his profits to exceed losses.

Once the stop is raised in order to cover commissions, the best thing to do is to avoid making it automatic from that point onwards. We should allow the market to develop its own stop or "signal" for it to be able to get out.

The problem with this land of a stop is how it can interfere with judgment. Here is a sample situation to explain it further. Imagine that there's a tall woman and then a short man trying to cross the street. Then, an automobile approaches. The woman believes that they have enough time to cross the street. However, her arm is held by the man who feels undecided to cross. He backs up and fills, pushes and then pulls her by the arm until they are back at the curb. It was a narrow escape. If she's to decide by herself, she would act according to what she knows is the right thing to do.

The same thing goes with the Tape Reader. His move is hampered when there is an automatic stop. He would be better off when he's free to act according to his own judgment. He shouldn't feel compelled to act based on a prior resolution to act under hard and fast rule.

Another instance when the stop order becomes significant to the Tape Reader is when his indications seemed to be defined not clearly. Of course, we need to make sure that the original commitment is made only when there is a positive indication in the trend. Situations, however, are expected to develop particularly during those times when he feels unsure whether he should stand pat, close out, or reverse the position he's currently in. During such time, it may be a better option to push the stop until it reaches a point that is as near as possible to the market price which should not choke off the trade as a result. This means that we should allow a reasonable area for temporary fluctuations. If the stock, which is uncertain beforehand, emerges and then goes towards an intended direction, we can assume the stock to change or to be cancelled. If, on the other hand, the trend seemed adverse, it is then closed automatically.

Note that hesitation, fear and uncertainty are the Tape Reader's deadly enemies. Primarily speaking, fear is caused by over-trading. Commitments should, therefore, be not greater than one's susceptibility that is inherent by birth. Hesitation on the other hand can be overcome if the individual performs disciplined self-training.

Observing a positive indication without acting on it is fatal which is even greater at closing than opening a trade. Once a definite indication has been determined, it should be followed immediately by an order.

Oftentimes, seconds have more value than minutes. We should remember that the Tape Reader does not assume the role of a captain but rather the engineer who is in charge of the machinery. The Tape should be considered as the pilot while the engineer should follow orders as promptly and as precisely as he could.

We have identified the Tape Reader as someone who follows the immediate trend. He is someone who pursues the line of least resistance. He follows the market and never bucks it.

The operator who displays an opposition to the immediate trend throws in his judgment and his several shares against the supply or demand of the world and its millions of shares.

Using a broom as a weapon, he tries to keep the incoming tide at bay. Should he decide to go with the trend, he should expect to see the forces of demand, supply, and manipulation to work for and with him.

When a market swings within a radius made up of a few points, it cannot be said to have a trend that is something that the Tape Reader should avoid.

The reason?

There's no way that he can pay commissions, accept occasional losses and then finally emerge on top unless he knows how to deal with the extremes of some minor swings. A yacht will not win in a dead calm. Since trading costs him almost half a point, each risk must have a probable two or five points profit. Otherwise, it is not justified. Take for example a mechanical engineer. If he knows the object's weight, the blow's force that strikes it, and the needed element to pass through, he can determine approximately the distance where the object will be driven.

The Tape Reader, upon learning the force or the energy when a stock starts and has the ability to sustain the movement, should be able to decide if it can move far enough to justify his choice to go with it – whether he sees it being able to pay its expenses and also being able to remunerate him for the simple reason of being bold in his actions.

On the other hand, an ordinary speculator who trades on tips earns one or two points in profit and never welcomes a loss though he can still get strangled if the loss happens to be big. The Tape Reader does the opposite. He should be able to cut out each possible eighth loss while at the same time find opportunities to make three, five and ten points. There's no need to grab everything which seemed to give an opportunity. He doesn't have to be constantly in the market either. He only chooses the best offer from the tape.

In time, the original risks he incurred can be eliminated through the useful arrangement of stop orders as soon as a stock goes his way. Either he keeps all these in the head or he places them down on the "floor." In my opinion, after carefully analyzing a danger point, I would seek to keep a mental stop. Then, upon seeing that the price has been reached, I would then close the trade "at the market."

The reason? Changing a plan or an opinion on short notice may be based on certain grounds. When the stop is on the floor, cancelling or changing it will definitely take some time. In other words, there are some moments when the operator has no idea on where he stands. If however, he uses mental stops and market orders, there's a chance that he would know where he stands, though this may not apply to the prices that he used when his orders were made. The main thing to consider is that he is aware whether he is in, or he is out.

When placing stops, note that doing so is most effective and scientific when it is indicated by the market. Let me show you an example:

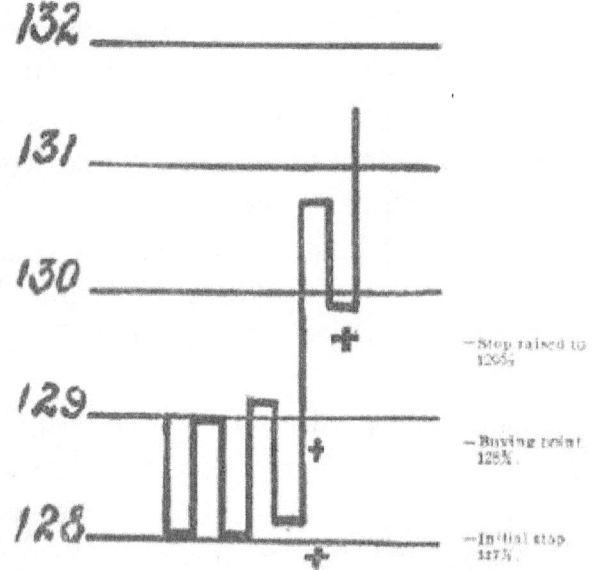

Notice that the stock here, which fluctuates between 128 and 129, shows a 128 ¾ buying indication. If such indication is correct, the price should not again break 128 since the buying seemed strong enough to turn it up two times from the given figure along with a third time from 128 1/8. Knowing that it did not land at 128 on the final downswing, we can then predict a higher upswing. It only tells us that the downward pressure was not strong enough; the demand is a little larger; and that it is more urgent. In short, the point of resistance was increased to 1/8.

Since we have set up the buying at 128 ¾, note that the stop is found at 127 7/8. This is ¼ lower than the last point of resistance.

The stock moves up higher than its previous top (129 1/8) and then it goes on to 130 ¾). Anytime after that when it crosses 130, there's a possibility that the traded increases his stop to cost plus commission (129). The stock will then respond at 129 7/8 and then continues to move on over 131. Once a new high point is achieved, note that the stop increases to 129 5/8 since 129 7/8 was the point of resistance on the dip.

If, for instance, the initial risk was 7/8 of a point with commission, etc., the market will then indicate a well-defined stop point, which means that an arbitrary stop is both unnecessary and expensive.

Though the illustration is shown in a chart form, an experienced Tape Reader normally keeps the swings inside his head. Several higher tops and bottoms that come in a series are seen in an obvious upswing while the reverse is seen in a down swing.

There's no way to fix a rule that is concerned about the amount of allowable profit to be accepted by the operator. Generally speaking, no limit should be set when it comes to profits. When a deal is made, it may seem as if it would gain three or four points. However, if there's an increase in the strength that comes with the advance, it should be able to run ten points before it gives a sign of halting.

You should remember at all times that the recommendations and suggestions given here are not to be treated as final or written on stone. We have no desire to act as an Oracle. What we are doing is we reason things out by the paper. As we go along and achieve a thing or two from these studies while using such tentative rules to the tape, you may find some opportunities in modifying a few of our reached conclusions when you are in an actual or paper trading.

A Tape Reader should decide to close a trade:

     1. when he gets an indication from the tape that he needs to close;

     2. when his stop ends up being caught;

     3. when his position seemed unclear;

     4. when his profit appears large or satisfactory that he wants to use the funds in order to gain better opportunities.

The number one and the most important reason for deciding to close a trade is:
It is what the tape is saying.

Such type of indication can be seen in a number of forms. If, for instance, the person is trading in a Leader stock, he should be able to notice the warning to come from the stock itself.
You may find that the recording of sales bears the smooth, silky thread of the trend. This can be very easy to see for someone who has a deep understanding of Tape Reading. Moreover, it is also very obviously seen in the leaders as explained by the reasons that have already been explained in the past.

If it so happens that the person is short of Union Pacific, and then all of a sudden the thread shows an indication of an upward shift in the market, it is then a foolish decision to choose to remain short. Apart from being compelled to cover quickly, if the movement's power is enough to ensure the risk, then the operator should go long. Being in a market that has enough breadth and swing, it is assumed that the Tape Reader realizes that when the trade should be closed, he should then reverse his position. Here, we can say that a person should have the flexibility of whalebone and be able to listen to non-rigid opinion.

His obligation is to comply implicitly to the tape. When closing a trade, an indication of which could come from a different stock, a number of stocks or the market in general. For instance, that day when the Supreme Court released its decision on Consolidated Gas, let's say that the operator was long of Union Pacific at 11 o'clock and paid 182 ¾.

At around 11 to 12 o'clock, Union rallied to 183 1/2/ while Reading, which is more active, rallied to 144. A little early than noon and immediately after, huge transactions happened in Reading. There were more than 50,000 shares switching hands in three-quarters of a point.
Most of these could probably be wash sales which come with inside selling. It's difficult to say. If not, we can say that at this level, there's a considerable buying power that was formed in Reading which was achieved by at least selling heavy enough in order to supply all bidders and to prevent the stock advancing more than 144 3/8.

Huge quantities of coining in a small range shows one of these things:

1. That at this point, there's a considerable buying power that suddenly developed. The insiders decide to check it or seize the opportunity to unload.

2. The demonstration in Reading could have been staged in order to distract attention from stocks wherein large operators were unloading. No special evidence can be traced except the one in New York Central.

When the selling seemed not enough to assess the upward move, we can say that the Reading market could have absorbed everything that was being offered and then move on to a higher level. In this case, however, selling, compared to buying, is more effectual. Reading, on its part, fell back, which serves as a reminder to the operator that the non-permanent leader on the market's bull side had succumbed to defeat. From this point, the operator begins to look for a slump.

In small lots, Reading went back down to 143 7/8. After selling at 183 5/8, Union Pacific declined to 183 1/4. These two stocks have shown dullness while the whole market became inactive in one way or another.

All of a sudden, Union Pacific dropped to 183 1/8. Then we see that UP went into trading of 500 shares at 183, 200 at 182 7/8, and 500 at 182 3/4. This shows that there is a lack of demand and poor support. Next in line is New York Central which, only a few minutes ahead, sold 400 shares at 131V2, came in 31 on 1700 shares, 130V4 on 500 shares and ended at 130 on 700 shares.

This only shows that the market was actually hollow and has the potential to develop great weakness. New York Central, which comes in large quantities and is at the low figure, has displayed, after being in a decline of a point and one half, that not only the supporting orders were missing but also the sellers have the duty to conduct great concessions for them to dispose their holdings. Such quantities, particularly when looking at how narrow the market is, only proved that these sellers should not be treated as small traders. Along with the wet blanket put on Reading as well as the unimpressive support in Union Pacific, such weakness in New York Central gives a glimpse of a future decline. With such indication of this land, note that the trader should be prepared to jump out of his long stock and then proceed with getting short of the market. During that time when he waits for his cue, the Tape Reader will have ample time to assess which stock among the leaders seemed most appealing for selling. He would then choose Reading on the basis that the huge lots which were distributed at around 144 are speculated to come into the market soon after some weakness develops.

The reason? Generally speaking, the investing public would normally buy on certain peaks which are similar to the ones that have taken place in Reading. Note that a huge volume, though it comes with a fractional advance, can make the ordinary trader strongly bullish. As a result, he nips off a number of long stock at the top of the market. Unaware as he may be, what he is doing is exactly what the manipulator wants.

We are aware about how people would boast on their purchase being at the top eighth while adding that such can turn the stock down. The people who make such purchases in this manner are the ones who get easily scared at the first hint of weakness which leads them later on to throw overboard their purchase. They are being manipulated by greed followed by fear.

Therefore, when the Tape Reader chooses Reading, he is picking out the stock where he would likely get the most help on the bear side.

At half past 12 pm, the market seemed to be standing still. At the same time, most of the transactions are in small lots while changes are only deemed fractional. Reading shows the result of unloading. It seemed to be coming out 500 at 143 ¾, 500 at 143 5/8, 400 at 143 1/2 and 400 at 143 ¾.

The operator learns that Reading is a short sale which has a stop order at 144 ½ or 5/8, the basis of which is that the bulls should have a special amount of buying power in order to push the stock over its former stop. Then, on every eighth advance above 144 3/8, they will meet some 50,000 shares. Such type of reasoning doesn't fall under our main argument, which, in fact, is to show how the hint in getting out of the stock will come from the action of stocks which are not being worked upon by the trader.

Union Pacific displays on the tape by small lots at 182 ¾; New York Central 1100 at 130, and 900 at 130 3/8. Everything else in the market seemed to have been stripped off all their snap and ginger and the operator showed no approval of his position on the long side.

He doesn't show any exact indication to sell short. He thinks that his chances on the long side have been decreased by the market's weak undertone. He then gets out of his Union Pacific and then waits until he is told by the tape to sell Reading short.

The Union Pacific weakens by 182 5/8. Others have slid off by a fraction. Aware that the weakness lacks enough strength to speculate any big break, he then decided to continue waiting. Shares of Union are determined as 182 5/8 altogether which is then followed by 3000 at 182 ½. Other stocks have reacted while the market itself seemed more bearish.

Consolidated Gas is said to trade at 163 ¾-163 ¼-163. Such is the first sign of activity found in the stock. However, such move is common for Gas since generally speaking, its fluctuations are wide and erratic. Looking at the balance of the list would give us a fraction. Gas trades 162 ½ to ¾ and then 500 at 162 ¼. From this point, Gas, which seemed to have been very dull right at this moment, would force itself, by its weakness and decline, based on the notice of the operator. He then starts looking at stock as potential shears, ready to cut the market thread and put everything down.

By 12:45 PM, Gas appears to be trading 500 at 161 ½. This seemed too weak. The list balance is steady, Reading 143 ¾, Central 130 3/8, Union Pacific 182 5/8. A fractional rally is also seen – Gas to 162 and Union Pacific to 182 7/8. There are plenty of Central for sale at around 130. Reading, on its part, is 143 ½.

The rally brings out gradual weakening on the whole. However, the Tape Reader is not able to go with the trend unless he feels confident of a big move. Trading at 129 ¾ is Central wherein it shows that after each and every buyer at 130 are filled up, sale of a considerable stock is still ongoing. Others are shown only in small lots. There is a looming decline in the market where a jar of any type will start to bring it down. At 182 ½, the Union Pacific seemed heavy. It trades 300 at 182 3/8, 200 at ½. Reading is at 143 ½, 3/8 while 1000 shares are at ½. Finally, Central trades 800 at 1/8 and 2000 at 130.

This is the thrust he has been searching for! Gas 163 ¾ on 200, ½ on 400, 161 on 300, 160 on 400! He immediately places an order on selling Reading short at the market. Everything seemed to be on the run now: Reading 143 ½, 600 at ¼, 1300 at ¼; Central 130, 129 ½, Gas trades 500 at 159 ½. There's something rotten about Gas which leads one to sell it short only if trading in a buzz-saw stock is tolerable.

Since the market breaks at a rapid rate, he is not able to get more than 142 ¾ for his Reading. However, he is short, as opposed to being far, from the top of what seemed like a hugely open break.

Everything seemed to be slumping at the moment – St. Paul, Southern Pacific, Smelters and Steel. Note that Union Pacific is down to 181 5/8 with the rest in proportion.

Gas is at 158 ½, 158 on 300, 157, 156, 155, 154, 153; all the others "come tumbling after." Reading 141 3/8, 500 at ¼, 400 at 141, 140 ¾, 500 at ½, 200 at 140, 600 at 139 ¾, 500 at 5/8. Union is at 181 to 180 7/8, ¾, ½, ¼, 600 at 1/8, 500 at 180, 179 ¾, 500 at ½, 300 at ¼; Central at 127 ½.

The given figures show how a Tape Reader's mind works. It also shows how a break in a stock which is purely foreign to where it is being traded in, will have an indication to come out and become short of one stock or more.

The indication of closing a trade could be sourced from the general market where we can see the trend as clearly developed all over the list and all stocks are working harmoniously. One of the top indications here is the strength or weakness on reactions and rallies.

Yes, it's true that the break in Gas, which touched 138 finally, was caused by the decision from the Supreme Court, the announcement of which came on the news tickers at 1:10 PM. However, just like any other case, the tape had spoken with the news several minutes before doing anything else. Such is one of the advantages of gathering news right from where it is reflected. Those who chose to wait for such information to reach them by telephone or by the roundabout way of word of mouth or news tickers are moving on a huge handicap.

Even the insiders did not know what the decision would be as shown by the dull state of the stock the whole morning.

People who have heard the decision made inside the chamber of the Supreme Court have gone straight, without having any doubt, to the telephone and decided to sell the stock short. The sales they made are displayed on the tape prior to the news' arrival in New York. Tape Readers were the ones that were notified first. They were short even before the Street knew what had transpired.

CHAPTER 7: UNDERSTANDING VOLUMES AND THEIR SIGNIFICANCE

Since the main focus of these studies is learning to read what the tape is saying, I am about to stress a point which is important to know and understand before we continue or else it would be difficult to clear up the explanations.

First, we need to know that the market for any type of stock and at any level is made up of two sides. These are the bid and the asking price.

Take note that the "last sale" is totally different from the "market price." If, for instance, Steel just sold at 50, such number represents what happened. We should think of it as part of history. Steel's market price is either 49 1/8 (0) 50 or 50 at 50 1/8. Putting together the bid and asked prices are what makes up the market price.

Such market price is comparable to a pair of scales. The volume of seller-thrown stock which purchasers have reached for determines which side has shifted momentarily.

As an example, let's say the tape shows the market price as 50 1/8. Then we take note that the large volumes belong to the up side. US 500 at 50, 1000 at 50 1/8, 200 at 50, 1500 at 50 1/8.

Here, we have four transactions wherein 700 shares are sold at 50 compared to 2500 that are bought at 50 1/8. This proves that at this point, the buying seemed more effective than the selling.

We can say that Steel may sell at 50 ¼ before 4g 7/8. Nothing is certain because supply and demand changes in every second. This is true not only in Steel but in every other stock that is found on the list.

This shows us one advantage when we trade only the leaders. We note that the influence brought by demand or pressure is first shown in the principal stocks.

The hand belonging to the one in a dominant position, whether he is an insider, a manipulator from the outside or the public, can be seen in these volumes. There is a simple reason for this. The big guys are not able to put up their stocks or even able to put them down if they don't trade in large amounts. Being in an advancing market, they are responsible of reaching up for their stocks or bidding up for it. Here is an example.

USD 1000 at 182 1/8;
200 at 182;
1500 at 182 1/8;
200 at 182 ¼;
3500 at 182 3/8;
2000 at 182 ½.

Do some opening trades coupled with subsequent transactions similar to the following:

200... 47 1/4	100...	45 7/8	100...	45 7/8
1900... 46 3/4	100...	46 1/8	100...	46
100... 46 5/8	100...	46	600...	45 7/8
100... 46 1/2	200...	46 1/4	500...	45 3/4

Note that the opening market price was set at 46 ¾, bid at 47 ¼ asking. Likewise, the buyers of 200 shares "at the market" opted to pay the high price. Bids at 46 ¾ were said to be filled. Proof of this is seen on the next scale set at 46 5/8. From there, the big lots are usually on the downside which only shows that pressure still exists. Therefore, the indications tell us that the stock would be decreased. Several 1900 shares in some stocks are said to be in a large quantity. However, in others, they are insignificant. Such points have a corresponding value and traders should be acquainted with them.

Volumes should be proportionate to the activity of the market and to the relative activity of that particular issue. There's no set rule that can be established. I know a Tape Reader, who can make money by following the lead of Northwest with its 1000 share lot where someone took at merely a fraction higher than the last sale. Normally, Northwest is a slow investment stock. This particular size lot seemed like the fore-runner of a type of demand that is both active and speculative. Let's try to find out what happens on the floor in order to come up with the above-described effect on the tape.

We shall now attempt to prove that the method we are using is correct.

Some years ago, the manipulation of a particular railroad was brought up at the New York Stock Exchange. They gave all the orders to a single brokerage house along with instructions on distributing such orders and concealing the buying as much as they can. The day's original order would say, "Take everything that is offered up to 38."

The number 38 was above the market by around 3 points the day before. This gave enough leeway for the broker who was entrusted with the buying order. He would then give his floor broker the following instruction:

"Last night, the stock closed at 35. What you should do is take everything that is offered up to 35 ½. Make sure that you give me a report on how things are standing. Never bid for the stock – simply take it when it is offered and then mark it down if you can."

In this particular case, we see that the floor member is standing in the crowd while he waits for the opening. The markets open, the chairman strikes his gavel; the crowd starts to yell. Someone was heard offering "Two Thousand at an eighth." Then, a different broker was saying "Thirty-five for five hundred." The broker in our story takes 2000 at 1/8. He then offers one hundred at one-eighth in order to keep the price down. Other people around him were also offering one or two hundred shares at 1/8 which makes him withdraw his offer. What he wants is to accumulate simply with the thought of offering or selling only when it would help him to buy more or to bring the price down. The buyer at 35 saw how the 300 shares of his lot were cancelled. This prompts him to change his bid to "thirty-five for two hundred." After receiving supply from other sellers, he then bids "7/8 for a hundred." The broker in our story sells him 100 at 7/8 for the sole purpose of getting the price down. Someone was then heard saying "a thousand at five." Hearing this, our broker then says, "I'll take it." Another five hundred is offered at 1/8 which he also takes just the same.

Let's take a closer look on how the tape records these transactions. We shall open 35. 2000 at 35 1/8; 200 at 35; 100 at 34 7/8; 100 at 35; 500 at 35 1/8.

On that day when the trader would interpret the transactions:

The bid at the opening and the asked price was 35 1/8. One person took the large lot (2000 Shares) at the high price.

The next two sales were in small lots and showed light pressure. The 100 at 35 after 34 7/8 shows that with the market of "7/8 bid" – "5 ask," the buyer decided to take the stock at the price offered and then followed up his actions by taking 500 more at the eighth. Here, the demand seemed dominant. It's not important if the buyer is a single individual or a dozen. Note that the momentary trend moves upward.

For us to get the opposite side, imagine that a manipulator wanted to depress a stock. He can do this by simply offering and selling more than the demand it gets. He can also coax or frighten other holders to throw their shares over. There's absolutely no difference in whoever's stock is sold. "The Lord is on the side of the heaviest battalions," goes the old adage. If, for instance, the manipulator places a broker into a crowd along with orders in order to mark it down, the broker then delivers all bids and then he offers it down until the desired point or until he meets the resistance that is too strong for him to overcome without losing a large block of stock.

We can say that the stock in question sells at around 80 while the broker's orders are to "place it up to 77." As we go further into the crowd, we see that he then finds 500 which was wanted at 79 7/8. He also finds 300 which was offered at 80. The last sale went with 100 at 80.

We can hear him shouting in the middle of the crowd: "I'll see you that five hundred at seven-eighths. A thousand or any part at three-quarters."

One broker was heard saying, "I'll take two hundred at three-quarters." A different voice was also heard saying, "A half for five hundred." "Sold!" somebody has responded. "A half for 500 more." "Sold!" "That's a thousand which I sold you at a half. Five hundred at three-eighths!" "I'll take a hundred at three-eighths," says another individual. He gets a reply. "You're on!" More replies are then heard. "Quarter for five hundred." "Sold!" The way he pounded the stock is revealed on the tape that went as follows:

Open 80.
500 sold at 79 7/8.
200 sold at 79 3/4.
1000 sold at 79 ½.
500 sold at 79 ¼.

If, for instance, there was strong resistance at 79, it would look something like this on the tape:

1000 sold at 79; 500 sold at 79; 800 at 79; 300 at 79 1/8; 1000 at 79; 500 at 79 ¼; 200 at 79 ½...

At 79, we can say that the demand was higher than what the individual was willing to supply. For instance, there could be 10,000 shares that are still wanted at 79 but it's more than what he could supply.

Often, a broker meeting like an obstacle will see itself leaving the crowd at a period that is long enough for one to call his principal. When he leaves, he paves the way for a rally because the stock is free from being under pressure while the huge buying order at 79 is used as a backlog for floor traders. This means that those who are from the crowd would place a bid of up to 79 ½ along with the hope of earning a fraction on the long side.

Let's look at a different case wherein two brokers are placed in the crowd. One is tasked to depress the stock while the other is to accumulate it. When they play, they do so into each other's hands. Then the tape delivers a report of what has happened in the following form:

Open 80 1/8 – 80.

200 at 79 7/8.

1000 at 79 7/8.

200 at 79 5/8.

500 at 79 ¾.

300 at 79 ¾.

1500 at 79 ½.

500 at 79 ¼.

100 at 79 1/8.

If we are on the floor, we should be able to see one broker who seemed to be offering the stock down while another was grabbing each round lot that he sees. There's no way for us to tell how far below the stock will be placed. However, when such indications appear, we decide to watch closely and wait for the turning point. Once this is realized, we would know that it is time for us to buy.

For the Tape Reader's part, it doesn't matter if the move is being done by a manipulator, by a group of floor traders, by the public, or everything combined.

The figures found on the tape shows a combination of an opinion consensus, manipulation effect, and the supply and demand. This is the reason tape indications are more dependable compared to what an individual hears, knows or thinks.

As the image of the pair of scales (supply-demand) becomes clear in our minds, we can take a look at the moment by moment transactions of the tape and weigh each indications in our mind in order for us to learn which side shows the strongest tendency. We shouldn't allow a single detail to be missed. When there's a sudden demand or a rush of liquidation, we may be able to form a new plan, change an old one or gain a neutral attitude.

Volume indications are usually not clear at all times. They are not infallible either. Simply relying on the indications of any single stock while excluding the rest will not do any good. Sometimes there are certain stocks that are run up. The volume indications shown in other active stocks tell us clearly that their distribution is as fast as the speed when the market takes them. Such occurrence happens a lot of times both on a small and large scale. It becomes more apparent at the turning point of a big swing wherein completing a distribution or accumulation would need several days. We can study volumes from the reports that are printed in the Wall Street Journal. The real method of studying them, however, is from the tape.

If, for instance, there's no way for you to spend five to seven hours at the tap when the ticker is being operated, you may opt to have the tape saved for you every day. This way, you would be able to study the tape at your leisure.

When we study under such conditions, make sure that it is done on a small scale. However, actual trades should be made with real money.

Sometimes, this rule on volumes shows almost the opposite of what had been explained beforehand. One such example was described in the previous chapter. Note that the transactions in Reading at such case suddenly bloated out of all proportion to everything else in the market at its own volume that it had previously. Taking into consideration the predominant element of apparent demand, the offered resistance (be it artificial or legitimate) became too overwhelming for the stock to overcome. Note that it also fell back from 144 3/8. As we move up, we can say that the volumes suggested a purchase. However, the tape displayed transactions at an abnormal level that comes with a poor response as given by everything else found on the list. The result is a smack of manipulation and a warning to the operator on being cautious on the bull side.

Even after a reaction came out from the stock, we can see that the large volume in Reading was retained. However, the huge lots were being thrown over towards the bid prices. Looking at the way up, we can see that the volumes were almost all on the up side while the small lots are seen on the downside.

After reaching 144 3/8, we see the large lots situated on the downside while the small lots are plotted on the up.

700 at 143 5/8.

500 at 143 ¾.

5000 at 143 5/8.

1700 at 143 ¾.

200 at 143 5/8.

4300 at 143 ¾.

3700 at 143 7/8.

100 at 144

12 PM.
500 at 144.
1300 at 143 7/8.
3000 at 144.
5000 at 144 1/8.
2100 at 144 ¼.
2200 at 144 1/8.
3500 at 144 ¼.
4000 at 144 3/8.
3000 at 144 ¼.
2500 at 144 1/8.
3500 at 144.
400 at 144 1/8.
1000 at 144.
500 at 144 1/8.
1100 at 144.
2000 at 143 7/8.
2500 at 143 ¾.
1000 at 143 5/8.

The turning point in Reading, morning of Jail. 4,1909 – the day when we see a collapse in the Consolidated Gas.
Studying small lots has the same importance as studying large lots.

We can compare the smaller quantities to the feathers found in an arrow. They show us that the business side of the arrow is found on the other end. In short, these smaller lots allow one to be constantly informed about the fraction that is formed on the other side of the market.

Say for example, in the Reading's first five trades that were recorded above, we can see the market quotation as being 5/8 at ¾; then it changes to ¾ at 7/8 and to 7/8 at 4. Moving downwards, it reaches 4 at 1/8. Notice how at this level, the small lots are important in indicating the pressure that was present.

Stocks such as Steel, Reading and Union would normally use a volume of 25,000 to 50,000 shares as a turning point. If, for instance, they are met with opposition beforehand or a decline, there must be a considerable quantity for it to be able to stem the tide.

As you walk into a hilly country, you may notice that there's a small river quietly running not far below. Such stream is so small that you can actually put your hand against its course and watch how the water backs up. Within only five minutes, the stream finds a way to overcome the resistance when you see it going over or moving around your hand. You would then go for a shovel, pile some dirt along its path, pack everything down and then utter the words, "There, I've damned you up." But such is not the final case after all. When you go back the next day, you would see that your pile of dirt was washed away. This prompts you to bring cartloads of dirt and then create a substantial dam. Finally, the flow was held in check.

The same thing goes with individual stocks or with the market. We can see that the prices follow the line that has the least resistance. When the Reading moves up, a person may throw 10,000 shares along its path without any perceptible effect. This is then followed by another lot of 20,000 shares. At this point, the stock halts although it eventually overcomes the obstruction. Then we see the seller giving another order wherein he throws 30,000 shares more on the market. If a total of 30,100 shares is needed at that level, all of the 30,000 are then absorbed by the buyer and we can see an increase in the stock. If, on the other hand, there are only 29,900 shares that are needed in filling all the bids, such price will go down because the demand was overcome by supply.

All of these seemed to have happened in Reading based on the referred occasion. It doesn't matter whether manipulative orders have predominated or not. This doesn't change the nature of the case.

Looking at the final test, we can see the weight being shown on the downside.

While the manipulator is doing his work, we notice that the public and the floor traders are not standing aside each other. The same is not true on the reverse. Each and everyone's stock looks similar on the tape.

Here is a good illustration of E.H. Harriman's work being regarded as an important turning point in Union Pacific.

A Volume Study in Union Pacific with 39,300 shares being supplied at 149 3A to 150, a closer look on the rise.

Once the stream was able to break through a dam, it finds itself inside a new territory. The same thing goes with breaking through a stock that is deemed as significant because it shows that the resistance has been surpassed. When there is a stronger resistance, it is less likely that further obstacles would be encountered in the immediate vicinity. Remember that dams are not built one behind the other. This means that in the case of stock, it is best that we go with it as we see one emerging into a new field. It is especially true when breaking through it means it would carry along the rest of the market.

Though we can learn a lot from the reports that have been printed in the daily newspapers that were mentioned previously, remember that moment by moment transactions-trades while they appear – is the only instruction book that is real. Here, a live tape is more preferred because the speed element involved in receiving information should be treated with huge concern.

We can use the comparative activity of the market based on peaks and breaks as our guide to the market's current technical situation. Say for example there is a decline. When the ticker becomes very active while the sales volume is seen as large, this indicates voluntary or compulsory liquidation. Such is emphasized on the next rally when the tape moves slowly and we can see only small lots. Looking at an active bull market, we note that the ticker seemed choked with the volumes of sales that are poured through it as shown by the advances. Looking at reactions, we note that the quantities and the number of impressions become lower until, just like the tile ocean on an ebb tide, the market appears almost lifeless.

We can see another indication that shows the power of a movement in the differences found between the sales of active stocks. Here is an example.

1000 at 180.

100 at 180 1/8.

500 at 180 3/8.

1000 at 180 ½.

We can see that only 100 shares are for sale at 180 1/8 while there is absolutely none at 180 ¼ and only 500 at 3/8. The leap from 1/8 to 3/8 indicates both the non-existence of pressure and the persistence of the buyers. They don't feel contented to wait patiently until they are able to get the stock at 180 ¼. What they do is simply "reach" for it. Looking at the opposite side of things would show us that some form of support is lacking.

When we judge an indication, we don't have to do it by the rule based on the conditions that surround it. The tape produces motion pictures in a continuous series along with their corresponding explanations given in between the printings.

These so-called "motion pictures" of the market use a type of language that is alien to all casual investors. However, to the Professional Tape Reader, they are comprehensible.

Several people who have read the past editions of this book have been misled by the ease involved in reading through volumes found in some market types. They have wrongly reached a conclusion that all that someone needs to do is simply sit beside a ticker and then watch the side where the volumes are on, whether it is the buying of the selling side.

This is where the mistake comes in. When we look at the exchange rule in the past, a buyer who wanted to exert an influence into the market through an upward movement could place a bid for 10,000 shares or any other number in big quantity. No other person would be able to sell him anything that is lesser than the quantity he is bidding for unless there is a willingness on the buyer's part to take it. Based on the existing rules, the buyer is expected to take any part from the 10,000 shares or whatever amount he bids for as long as he doesn't indicate "all or none" to his broker.

The change in the rules, along with the other restrictions made against manipulations, matched orders, etc., can eliminate a huge amount of transactions in large quantities either at the advanced or at the decreased price. It came from an old trick of Harriman's together with some of the previous Standard Oil party and other minor manipulators and floor traders to produce these offers and bids in round lots while another individual supplies or takes them for their effect on the market. However, such change in the rules has caused the volume to be immensely reduced, and the value of indications decreased. So, while they are still being too suggestive to a tape reader with an observant character and so long as the principle remains unchanged, it is not a good thing to depend on them fully.

Such volumes that have been under our discussion seemed least liable to mislead during such time when manipulation prevails. This is because the manipulator has the responsibility to deal in huge blocks of stock and has to be able to show his hand continually. A full manipulative operation seen on the long side is composed of three parts:

1. Accumulation;
2. Marking up; and
3. Distribution.

For a shorting operation, note that the distribution appears first, followed by the marking up and finally the accumulation. Not one of these three parts can be complete with the absence of the other two.

The manipulator should be able to work with a huge block of stock or else the deal would be worthless of his time, expenses and the risk. The Tape Reader should be able to execute operations on either side of the market. When it comes to accumulation, it will appear in the quantities and in the manner that they appear on the tape. He decides not to buy it at once since he knows that it may take weeks or months before the manipulator finally completes the accumulation of his line. Moreover, there could be opportunities in buying cheaper. By putting things off until that moment when he forces another to carry the stock on his behalf in order to pay his interest. Lastly, his capital remains free temporarily.

As soon as the marking upstarts, he places himself in the commencement of the move. He carries on until he sees signs of a halt or distribution. After passing through the first two periods, he earns the position of benefitting fully from the third phase of the operation.

At this point a figure chart, which was discussed in a different chapter, will aid the trader, particularly if the manipulative operation is carried on within a certain period of time. This will definitely provide a bird's eye view of the deal which in turn will allow him to either drop or resume the thread at any given stage.

CHAPTER 8: Understanding Market Technique

On the morning of February 27, 1909, a Saturday, the market opened a little higher than the close of the previous night.

Reading was seen as the most active stock. After it has touched 123 ½, it then went down to 122 ½ wherein it invited short sales. Such indication was later on emphasized at 122, at 121 ½, and then lastly at 121. Note how the downward trend was heavily marked until it hit 119 7/8. Afterward, it followed a quick rally of 11/8 points.

Such was a vicious jab of three points found in a market that was on the early stage of recovery from a decline back in early February.

You may ask what effect it can have to other principal stocks. In Union Pacific's case, it declined at a mere ¾, Steel at 5/8 and Southern Pacific at 5/8. This only shows that technically speaking, they were strong. In other words, they were in a position which could see, coupled with equanimity, a three-point break based on a leading issue.

If such drive happened when the Reading was at about 145 and the Union was at 185, its effect on the others should be somewhat different.

In order to measure the extent of an ore body, miners would have to use a diamond drill. This results to a core wherein its character is shown based on what is found underneath the surface. If, from the very beginning, we are able to drill into the market from the top, we should be able to see that the bulk of the floating supply in Reading, Steel and others was kept by a class of traders who usually purchase heavily in booms and by bulge. Normally, these people move with small margins, experience, and nerve. They are really vulnerable which means that the stocks in which they operate would experience the biggest declines if the market get ajar. The next figures look interesting.

1907-9 Advance	Feb, '09 Decline	Break to Advance
U.P. 14.7%	84¼	12 3/8
Reading 33.6%	73¼	26 3/8
Steel 44.6%	36¼	16 1/2

The figures above tell us that the public seemed strongly extended in Steel; a little less loaded with Reading, and was carrying too small with Union Pacific. In short, Union displayed technical strength through its resistance to pressure. With Reading and Steel, on the other hand, there is little or no opposition given to the decline.

Both the market and the individual stocks ought to be judged according to what they do and to what they do not do base on critical areas.
If the big individuals who gained Union lower than 120 had distributed it over 180, it would cause the stock to break into something like 30 points because it had been passed on from strong to weak hands. Since there was no such decline but just a very minute reaction as compared to its advance, the Tape Reader says that the Union is meant for bigger prices; that it brings immunity from declines and possibly a large advance in the not-so-distant future.

Even if the Union Pacific was meant for a thirty-point rise in the coming two weeks, something can occur that would postpone the campaign for some time. The Tape Reader, however, should work with these wider considerations fully. He only has so much time and capital which he should employ in order to earn the biggest results. If, after watching the most favorable opportunities, he can begin to work with the trend in a stock, some day or even week, it will show him ten points profit which is more than any other issue on hand and increasing his chances to some extent.

A long advance or decline normally culminates by the leaders' wide and quick movement.

Let's look at the break of February 23, 1909: There was a decline of 118 from 128 ¾ in Reading and 41 ¼ from 46 in Steel, which happened in a single day. Southern Pacific, which moved up from 97 to 112, reached a climactic seven-point jump within one session.

Instances are so many that citing them are hardly worth it. This also applies to the market as a whole – a movement that is exceptionally violent, after it has gone through a protracted sag or rise, usually hints termination.

Generally speaking, a stock shows the Tape Reader what it wants to do based on its action under stimulation or pressure. Say for example that on Friday, February 19, 1909, an announcement came from the United States Steel Corporation, which talked about an open market in steel products. Such news later came out in the open.

In the morning, the news was heard by everyone in the country. The Tape Reader, after weighing the situation prior to the next day's opening, would exclaim – "As the news is public property, the normal thing for Steel and the market to do is to rally." He further added that Steel closed the previous night at 48 3/8 and that the market seemed to hinge itself upon such singular stock.

Note that the opening price of U.S. Steel was down from the past closing by three-quarters of a point. Such is a perfectly natural occurrence if we look back at the announcement. This will then be followed by the real test of strength or weakness. Within the first ten minutes, Steel shows these figures on the tape:
200 at 47 7/8.
4500 at 47 ¾.
1200 at 47 7/8.
1500 at 47 ¾.
...No variations are apparent. Note that the price swings back and forth within the same fractions for a number of 18 times.

In the meantime, Union Pacific, after opening at 177 ½, shows the possibility to rally and pull up the rest of the market behind it.
The question is: Do you think that Union can lift Steel? Here, we can see two opposing forces. See how the Tape Reader watches just like a hawk because he is "going with the market" towards the direction of the trend. Union is up 7/8 since the opening while the Southern Pacific reinforces it. However, Steel

does not respond. It never got out of the ¾ - 7/8 rut. There's not a single hundred share lot that could be sold at 48. In other words, it is being offered freely at 47 7/8. It also has no rallying power despite the leadership executed by the Harriman's. Union, on its part, seemed to be inducing the following as a final effort: 2000 at 178 ½

----Steel responded by breaking through with a punch:

800 at 47 5/8.

Such is the Tape Reader's cue to do short. In just a short span of time, he has placed Steel in such a way that he gets 47 ½ or 47 3/8 since there are huge volumes that were traded in using such figures.

Union Pacific looks disheartened. It feels the Steel millstone hanging heavily around its neck. It goes down to 178 ¾, ¼, 1/8 and finally to 177 7/8.

Steel feels the pressure as it increases at the low level. The following shows the successive sales that are made.

6800 at 47 ½.

2600 at 47 3/8.

500 at 47 ¼.

8800 at 47 1/8.

From this point onwards, we see a steady flow of long stock found all over the list. We can see that Reading and Pennsylvania are weakest among the railroads. Colorado Fuel has broken seven points as it goes through a decline while the other steel stocks follow just the same. U.S. Steel is dumped too much at the bidding. Even something that is deemed as dignified is also affected.

After the two-hour session, we see that the market closes underneath wherein Steel was at 46 which left thousands of accounts vulnerable because of the decline and a looming holiday for holders to be worried about.

The Tape Reader may have the notion that the stock would go lower on the next Tuesday that follows. If, for instance, no covering indication is seen, and unless he has an invariable rule to close each trade every day, he then decides to place a stop at 47 on short Steel and then go his way. Originally, his stop was 48 1/8.

Steel decides to open the session at 44 ¾ at ½. During the day, it makes a low record of 41 ¼.

We can learn a number of lessons from this episode. Tape reading can be successful with the study of Force. An individual should have the capacity to judge which side has the biggest pulling power. Then, he should have the courage to go with that side. Critical points can occur in each swing, similar to the life of a business or of a person. Based on these junctures, we can assume that a feather's weight placed on either side is enough to determine the Critical trend.

Anyone who knows how to find these points certainly has a lot to win and little to lose. This is because he can always play with a stop that is placed near behind the turning point, otherwise known as the "point of resistance." If Union carried on with its upward course and then it gains in power, influence and volume as it progresses, it may help in overcoming the negative effects brought by the Steel situation. It was based simply on the question of power. At this point, we can say that Steel has pulled Union down.

Studying the "responses" to stimulation or the stocks' outside influences is one of the most important aspects in the education of the Tape Reader. It is an almost perfect guide to the market's technical position. It's true however that all responses are not defined as clearly as they should be.
Concerns such as who or what produces these tests or those periods that are critical is simply a thing of indifference to the Tape Reader. These things regularly appear and disappear. Therefore, he should be able to give a diagnosis and act accordingly. When a stock is controlled higher, seldom do we expect the movement to continue unless this is followed by the other stocks which then support the advance, blocking certain developments that are affecting a stock, all the other issues should be observed in order to see if large operators are unloading on those spots that are strong.
If a stock fails to break on bad news, insiders would have anticipated about the decline and then seemed ready to buy.

Normally, the tape shows what this is. One magazine had once showed that Rock Island, at one day in August, preferred to have been driven down to 28 along with rumors on receivership. The waiter mentioned in the article failed to prove that such rumors were started by the insiders because he had admitted on his part that during such time when the transactions were made, they were not fully understood.

Maybe they seem inscrutable to someone who lacks the experience in tape reading. However, we remember too well that the indications seemed to be all in favor of buying the stock while on the break. Such transactions were too large, and they seem to be out of every proportion to the floating supply and the capital stock outstanding.

So, what does this mean to the Tape Reader? There are thousands of shares of stocks that are traded in every day, after a small rally and a ten-point decline. If the sales volume indicated long stock, there is someone who will buy it. If manipulation is present, it is not for the purpose of distributing the stock at a low level. This means that by simply casting out those factors that are unlikely, it would be easy for the Tape Reader to arrived at a conclusion that is correct.

The market is being subjected to the test regularly by a single element, the mention of which has been little, i.e. the floor traders. These people are always on the alert to hunt a weak spot in the market because of their love for the short side.

If a lack of support is detected in an issue, it will then lead to a raid which, thinking that the technical situation seemed weak, will then spread to the floor's other parts and creates a reaction or a slump all around. If, however, they find a short vulnerable interest, they should be able to quickly bid up a stock and then drive the shorts in order to cover. Considering all these and the other operations that are happening all the time, the Tape Reader, believed to be an expert, will rarely be confused in discerning which side lies his best chances. Other people seemed to be doing those which he would do by himself assuming that he was all powerful. Though it is the smaller swings that interest him most, the day trader should not fail to maintain his bearings according to the wider movements of the market.

When there's panic, he acknowledges it in the birth of a bull market. He then operates under the certainty that prices will increase gradually until it reaches a boom towards the extreme of the swing. Being in a bull market, he would think that reactions that come from two to five points are fairly normal and reasonable. He searches for occasional fall of 10 to 15 points in the leaders along with a 25-point break for at least once in every year. If any of these take place, he would know what he should look for next. Moreover, at the bull market, he would expect that a fall of 10 points would be followed by a recovery of around half of the decline. If, then, the rise would continue, all of the fall and even more will be recovered. When the stock or the market didn't want to rally naturally, he then understands that the trouble was not overcome yet. This would prompt him to look for a further decline.

Let's take a look at American Smelters, which achieved a top of 99 5/8 some years ago. Then, they slumped off according to rumors of competition and reached 78. Covering indications were shown at around 79 ½. Should the operator had gone long, he may have expected Smelters to rally to around 89. The decline, which was seen at 21 5/8 points, led to a rally of 10 ¾ points.

For record's sake, the stock had recovered to 89 3/8. Sure, these things are simply guided posts since the Tape Reader's actual trading is performed only on the most positive and promising indications. They are, of course, significant in teaching him what he needs to avoid. For example, he would be careful about initially making a short sale of Smelters following a 15-point break despite the fact that his indications were clear. There could be a number of points more on the short side but then he realizes that each point that it declines further brings him nearer to the turning point. Then, after the said violent break, he realizes that the safest way to earn some money is by waiting for an opportunity on the long side.

Let's take a look at a different scenario. Say, for instance, Reading sold on January 4, 1909, at 144 3/8. Towards the end of the month, it reached 131 ½. Then on February 23, it broke ten points to 118.
This shows us a decline of 24 3/8 points (assuming that a 2 percent dividend was paid). Like what has been stated before, the stock appeared like an attractive short sale. This is true not only on the initial breakdown but also on the final drive. For the conservative trader, he would have waited for a buying indication since less risk is expected on the long side.

It is rare for a market to run for over three or four consecutive days in a single direction with no reaction. The Tape Reader should then realize that his chances get smaller as the swing is sustained.

Daily movements normally offer the best opportunities. He should, however, keep in stocks that swing wide enough in order to secure himself a profit. Napoleon has once said, "The adroit man profits by everything, neglects nothing which may increase his chances."

An average outside speculator uses methods that don't seem to offer much of an improvement to this. This explains why a lot of people lose their money.

As an expert, the Tape Reader is against such people and their methods diametrically speaking. When he angles for profits, he would apply science and skill.

He would then study, figure things out, analyze profusely, and then deduce. He understands exactly where he is, what he has been doing, and why he's doing them.

CHAPTER 9: Dull Markets and the Opportunities They Bring

A number of people would think that a dull market is a problem as far as trading is concerned. They would exclaim, "Our hands are tied; it's impossible for us to get out of what we have; if we could, it's useless to decide getting in once again since no matter what we do, we can't make a dollar."

These people are not authentic Tape Readers. They are, in fact, Sitters.
The truth is; dull markets bring some opportunities. We only need to dig underneath the crust of prejudice in order to find them.

The presence of dullness in the market or in any other stock tells us that those forces which can influence it in such direction that is either upward or downward have reached a balance on a temporary basis. The best way to illustrate this is by using a clock that is soon to run down. The clock's pendulum gradually decreases the swings' width movement until it reaches a full standstill, as illustrated by this:

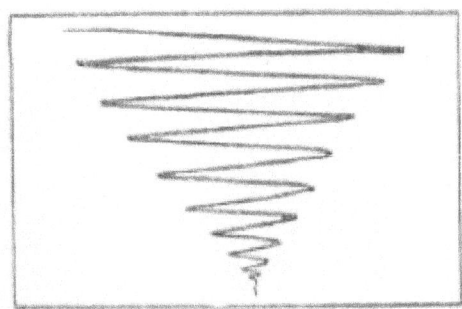

How the market pendulum comes to a standstill

When you turn this diagram sideways, you will see how the chart of a market or a stock appears like upon reaching the point of dullness:

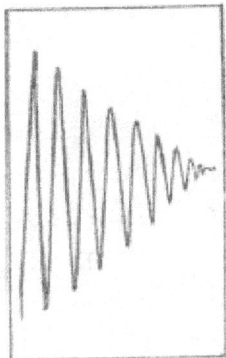

Dull periods like these usually occur after a season of hyperactivity on the bull side. People would make money, do pyramiding on their profits, and then glut themselves with the stocks on top. Once everyone else becomes loaded up, there is no one who is left to buy. A break could occur if no bears are present and that there are no bad news or anything else that would push for a decline.

Nature offers its solution for dissipation. She brings the debauch together with its start, its climax, and then its downfall along with a throbbing head and a carpet tongue. This allows him to remain silent until a repair for the damage is presented. The same goes with the intervals of market rest. Traders who have positioned themselves to be trimmed would be trimmed duly.

What happens next is that they lose their money while also losing their nerve temporarily. Therefore, we can say that market becomes neglected. Here, we see that extreme dullness has settled in.

If there's a need to write the history of the market, such periods of lifelessness should be marked at the end of each chapter. This is because those factors that were active in creating the main movement, together with staid, climax and collapse, have used up their force.

Therefore, we can say that prices would settle into a groove. Here, they remain for weeks or until they become affected by some powerful influences. When a market sees itself being in the midst of a large move, there's no way for anyone to tell how long or even how far it will continue to run. When prices become stationary, however, we learn from this point that a swing will be pronounced in one direction or another.

In reality, there are ways to anticipate the swing's direction. The first one is by understanding the technical strength or weakness present in the market which has been discussed in a previous chapter. The act of resisting a pressure that is said as something that was seen during the dull period of March 1909 was followed by a rise. This prompted the stocks to sell several points higher. This was especially true in the case of Reading wherein such shakeouts around 120 (one of such had been described) were positive and had occurred frequently. In the case of insiders, when they shake other people out, it only means that they solely want the stock themselves. Such time is a perfect time for us to enter.

If a dull market cannot hold rallies, or if it has no ability to respond to bullish news, it only shows that technically speaking, it is weak. Until something comes up to alter the situation, the next swing will definitely be downward.

On a different note, if there is a gradual hardening in prices; if the bear raids weren't able to dislodge acceptable quantities of stock; and when stocks do not show any movement of decline when the news is unfavorable, we could perhaps look at an advancing market in the not-so-distant future.

There's no way of telling whether a dull market will eventually merge and then turn into being a very active one. As such, the Tape Reader should be on the watch at all times. It is then considered as foolish for him to exclaim: "The market is dead dull. There's no use to watch it today. Just a mere sub point was swung by the leaders yesterday. There's nothing utterly profitable that can occur in such type of market."

This type of reasoning is bound to make one miss the best opportunities – those of Seeing one's self on the ground floor of a big step ahead.

Let's say that during the accumulation mentioned previously in Reading, the stock had a range of between 120 and 124 ½. With no warning, it suddenly gave an indication (around 125) that the absorption had been concluded and that the stock had started to advance.

Since the Tape Reader had explained beforehand that such accumulation should not be treated as a small investors game, he would then grab a bunch of Reading once the indication shows up. Perhaps he had bought more than he wanted for purposes of scalping, along with the intention of keeping some part of his line for a long swing. He then uses the rest for the purpose of regular trading.

As the stock moves away from his purchase price, he may have simply raised his stop on the lot that he plans to hold, adding some mental label to it under the effect that it should be sold only if he detects inside distribution. He then gets the chance to benefit to the fullest through any manipulative work that he could have done. In short, he says: "I will be able to get out of this lot once the big boys and their big friends got out of theirs."

He feels some ease in his mind regarding the stock since he has observed the accumulation and realizes that it has relieved the market of every floating supply at such level. This goes to show that a sharp, quick rise is expected sooner or later since there is a little stock to deal with on the way up. If, by chance, he has neglected to watch the market regularly and then he gets in from the very start, his chances would be greatly decreased. Perhaps he wouldn't have the courage to take on the bigger quantity.

Friday, March 26, 1909
Reading and Union were deemed as dull as two leaders could be. Reading opened at 132 ¾. It went high at 133 ¾, low at 132 ¼, and last at 132 5/8. In Union's case, it saw an extreme fluctuation at 5/8 – reaching 181 ¼ from 180 5/8. Activity was seen as being confined to Kansas City, Southern, Beet Sugar, etc.

The next day, Saturday, the opening offered every indication that the dullness shown on the previous day would occur once again. Initial sales display changes only at a fractional level.
Let's look at this example. B. & O., Missouri Pacific, and Wabash pfd were up ½ or 3/8. Union was higher by 1/8 while Reading was lower at 1/8.
Beet Sugar was down at 5/8 and sales were at 32. Reading indicated 1100 at 132 ¼, 800 at 3/8, Union 800 at 181, 400 at 181, 200 at 181 1/8, 400 at 181. One hundred Steel was at 45 ½, 1/8. B&O is 100 at 109 7/8. The market is dead having lots that are mostly single 100 share.

Now we arrive at our cue! Reading 2300 at 132 ½, 2000 at ½, 500 at 5/8. Such quantities that are taken at the offered prices tell us only one thing. The Tape Reader than takes on a lot of Reading "at the market."
Whatever is going on in Reading, everything else in the market seemed slow to respond. However, N.Y. Central appeared like it is willing to help even a little – 500 at 127 ½ (after ¼). Beets are then up to 33 ¼. Steel is at 45 1/8 while Copper is at 77 ¼ which is better by the fraction.

Reading 300 at 132/2. Steel 1300 at 45 1/8, ¼.
Union 100 at 181.
Reading 300 at 132 5/8.
Beets 100 at 33 ½. Union 700 at 181 ½.
N.Y. Central 127 5/8, 600 at 3/5…7/8!…
Some help are coming!
Union 900 at 181 ½; now Reading 100 at 132 ¾. Copper 700 at 71 ½.
Reading 800 at 132 7/8, 100 at 133, 900 at 133, 1100 at 1/8…
Reading 1500 at 133 ¼, 3500 at 133 ½…there's not that much doubt on the trend at this point.

The market, as a whole, is deemed as responding to Reading. There is also a steady increase in volume, breadth and power. Such rapid advances tell us that short covering should not be regarded as a small factor. It also appears like several people are throwing their Beet Sugar as they get into the big stocks. Smelters and St. Paul Copper start to lift a bit.

A short period of hesitation was seen at 11 AM wherein the market appears to take a long breath as it prepares for a next effort. It is rare to find any reaction while no weakness can be seen either. Reading on its part, backs up to 133 ¼ by a fraction while Union was up to 181 3/8.
No selling indications can be seen. This means that the Tape Reader stands by his own guns. At this point, however, they seem to be picking up again…
Reading 133 3/8, ½, 5/8, 3A…Union 181 5/8
N.Y. Central 128 ½, 1/8, 700 at 1/4.
Union 1000 at 181 ½, 3500 at 5/8, 2800 at 7/8, 4100 at 182, Steel at 45 ½…

From here until the close, everything is nothing but bull, and everything closes according to a fraction of that which is highest. Reading reaches 134 3/8, Union 183, Steel 46 1/8, Central 128 7/8, and then the rest, according to proportion.
Since the market earned such headway, it will take some strong news to halt a high and wide opening on Monday. The Tape Reader, for his part, has the choice of either closing things out at the high point or putting things in a stop as he takes his chances over Sunday.

At this point, we can figure out the advantage of watching a market that is deemed as dull and then getting into that moment when it begins to go out of its rut. We could almost plot the lines on the chart of a leader such as Reading or Union (the upper line shows the high point of its single-tone swing while the lower line deals with the low point)and then buy or sell every time that line gets crosses. **This is because when a stock has shaken itself loose from a radius that is narrow, it is apparent that the distribution, accumulation or resting spell had a wrap-up and new forces are seen at work.** Such forces are the most effective and pronounced at the onset of a new move – there is more power needed when starting a thing compared to when we keep things going.

There are some readers who may think that the illustrations are being given after such things occur on the tape. Moreover, they may think that what the Tape Reader did during such time was problematic.

I would then like to clarify that my tape illustrations are sourced from the indications which had revealed themselves that time when they were printed fresh on the tape. During such period, I had no idea of what is going to happen.

There are several other ways that a trade could choose to employ himself on dull periods. One of these is by keeping tap on the leaders' points of resistance and then play on these for profits that are fractional. We admit, at this point, that such occupation is rather precarious. This is because the operating expenses make up a really heavy percentage against the player. This is particularly true when the leading stocks swing just by a single point or so for every day.

If, however, one chooses to take such chances instead of being idle, the best way to do it is by keeping a chart where every fluctuation would be recorded.

This gives us a picture of what is happening. It also clearly outlines the areas of resistance and the momentary trend.

In the next chart, we see that the stock opens at 181 ¼ while the first point of resistance was at 181 ½. The initial indication that there's a downward trend can be seen in the dip to 181 1/8. Given that these two straws display some tendency, the Tape Reader then goes short "at the market," wherein he would get perhaps 181 ¼ (let's consider the worst part).

After doing a second unsuccessful attempt to break the resistance at 181 ½, we see the trend as turning downward. This is shown by the series of lower tops and bottoms

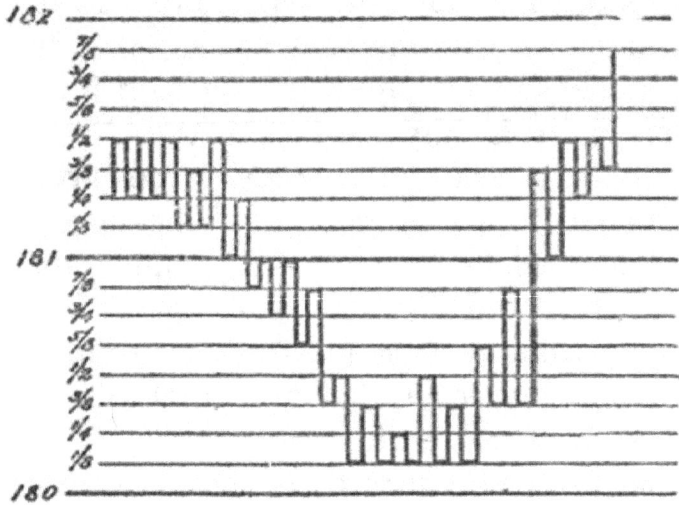

wherein the position is seen in an instant. When he opts to do nothing, he is suspected of being a guesser. If he decides to play under this plan, he should avoid mixing it with other ideas. Note that such method is solely applicable to a type of market that is very dull and, like what we have said before, is a type of business that is utterly precarious.

Therefore, we cannot recommend it.

As a rule, it will not do the Tape Reader any good when he attempts to scalp fractions out of the leaders found in a dull market. Taxes, commissions, the invisible eighth, along with frequent losses, are all considered as contributing to a handicap. There should be wide swings if profits would leap ahead of losses. The right approach at this point is to wait for good opportunities to arrive.

The saying "The market is always with us" is old and true. We shouldn't feel compelled to trade. Results should not be based on how often we trade but rather on how much money that we make. Another way of reversing a dull market into a good account is by trading in the stocks that are temporarily active which could be caused by the manipulative or other causes.

The Tape Reader does not give weight to the type of label that was placed on the goods. You can call a stock "Harlem Goats preferred" if you wish. Then, make such stock active by way of manipulation. This will cause the agile Tape Reader to trade in it in order to gain profit. He doesn't really mind if it's a railroad or a shooting gallery; if it declares regular or "Irish" dividends; if the abbreviation is A B C or C B A – as long as it brings indications and a wide liquid market where one can get in and out.

Let's take Beet Sugar on March 26, 1909. This is the day when Reading and Union were so dull. Beating Beat Sugar was rather easy. Even a Tape Reader that is still in an embryo would have made it long at 30 or even below. Moreover, since it never left him in doubt, he could simply have dumped it at the top prior to the close or he could have hold on to it until the next day when it touched 33 ½.

In the morning of March 5, 1909, we note that Kansas City Southern was drifting between 42 ¾ and 43 ½. Then, a little afternoon, the stock suddenly burst into activity along with large volume. Could there be a sane person who had thought that a hundred or even more individuals were convinced that Kansas City Southern seemed like a purchase at that instant?
Perhaps the rise could be attributed to the placing of manipulative orders where purchases had predominated.

Hence, the sudden activity, along with the volume and the advancing tendency prompted the Tape Reader to "get aboard." The manipulator then put out his hand while the "get aboard" Tape Reader would only need to go long with the current.
Not only was the advance sustained, it was also emphasized at some points. At this point, the Tape Reader could have resorted to pyramiding. He does it by using a stop that is near behind his average cost and brings it up in order to conserve profits. If, for instance, he had bought his first lot at 44, his second one at 45, and his third lot at 46, he could have simply thrown 46 5/8 as a whole and then achieve a net of $406.50 on that same day if he was using 100 share units during trading or $2, 032.50 if he was trading in 50 share units.

Chapter 10: Strategies on Effective Day Trading to Live By

Since the market these days are increasingly volatile, the way to survive in stock trading depends on the type of trading system that you have set up for yourself. Anyone who is a seasoned stock trader will tell you that no single foolproof way to protect yourself from losing money is available in this everyday trade. No matter if you choose to adhere to complex or simple rules is purely up to you because neither of which can guarantee profitability. Strategies in day trading, particularly for beginners, are usually hit-and-miss. As time goes by, you will earn the skills to read signals on when the timing is perfect for purchasing and for selling.

For you to succeed in day trading, you should be able to keep some strategies in mind. You should keep them as close to your heart as possible and think of it as your day trading mantras.

Day Trading Courses

Remember not to believe everything thoroughly what they tell you. It's true that it is helpful and convenient to be able to use software that would help you out when you are trading. However, you shouldn't allow such to perform all the thinking on your behalf. Perhaps, it may give you an objective view on how you should go about with your day trading but this should not stop you from making a personal analysis and from studying what is really going on with your trading during the day.

Analyze Your Mistakes

There's a saying that goes, "You win some, you lose some." If the latter happens, you should think about going back and reviewing your mistakes in order for you to prevent them from happening again. If you look back on the steps you made and then realize what went wrong, you will gain the knowledge of anticipating familiar issues in the future. You would also, of course, be able to avoid making the same mistakes. This is important if you really aspire on becoming a successful day trader.

When Common Sense Becomes Uncommon

Perhaps you have noticed that common sense has, sadly speaking, become a little uncommon at present. Rules that are the most simple and basic sometimes become the hardest to live by. For instance, everyone is aware that when a person wants to succeed in any kind of endeavor apart from stock trading, he must be very willing to put in those long hours. He should have strong work ethic, a thorough understanding on risk and money management, and more. In today's trading system, the problem is that everyone else is seeking for the shortcut, wanting to get big bucks while exerting little effort. Simply put, it doesn't work out in such way.

What then is exactly the best way to do when making decisions. These decisions should be informed decisions. Never allow emotions such as fear or anxiety block you from making smart choices. Such is the reason why you need to invest on education. Gather online resources, books, forums and do some research on the latest tools, trends and strategies on trading and investment. Any useful bit of information that you can get your hands on is surely a great help.

Get the Best of Both Worlds

It's purely okay to learn through the hit-and-miss tactic. Through this, you will learn as a first-hand experience, what method works and what does not. In the long run, you would be able to predict certain events even before they occur. Perhaps mastering such skill may take years but a number of experienced traders stress that this is the best way to do things. Another thing you can do is by looking for a mentor who has been there and has done that and then came out with success on his hand. Getting to know his insights may save you some money, time and future headaches. Of course, you can also choose to do both options.

There is no such thing as a perfect formula to make day trading strategies for you to earn millions of dollars all through your lifetime. Trading is similar to gambling. If you are not playing, then you are not winning. You should be able to learn how to embrace losses with as much grace as you can give to success. Only people who show willingness in taking risks and doing some sacrifices have a great chance to hit it big.

At this point, you have learned about the following:

- The meaning of day trading
- What day trading is all about
- The needed tips and tricks to learn
- The strategies that one has to employ
- Pitfalls that should be avoided

Now that you have a good understanding of the ones that were mentioned above, it's now time to learn about what you should do when there's a market decline.

Chapter 11: Day Trading for Beginners, its Do's and Don'ts

While the technicality and the high-strung lingo may seemed intimidating to a newbie, day trading for beginners shouldn't be really perceived as being complicated as long as you are willing to dedicate some of your time trying to understand the ins and outs of the process. Just like any endeavor, the chances to meet failure can be put at a minimum if you arm yourself with the right information and strategy to succeed.

With these in mind, let me now give some helpful tips that would help you navigate your way through day trading for beginners.

Be Able to Understand What Day Trading Is Really All About

Know that in here, stocks, bonds, and other forms of financial assets are being bought and sold all through the day by using a certain system. All of the items that were purchased correspond to the sales. You can see the profits or deficits by looking at the discrepancies between the goods and their corresponding trade prices. In day trading, the concept involves being able to finish all the transactions that were made before the end of the day in order to you to be assured that the closing price of your goods shall remain the same. Always remember that changes usually happen at night.

Be Able to Take This on a Serious Note, Particularly Since You're Just Starting Out

Never allow yourself to be carried away by the simplicity the principles in day trading. Never make any foolish assumptions since doing so will make you lose a lot of money. You can take calculated risks but do not simply rely on your guts. You should carefully study what's going on all through the day to avoid making hasty decisions which you will eventually regret.

Be Able to Know What To Do Every Time You Lose

It's fairly impossible to engage oneself in day trading without encountering losses every now and then. What is more important is that you know very well how you could regain the losses. Stop dwelling on the past. Only remember on not making the same mistakes again which had cost you a lot in the first place. You should aim to make a positive change and then move on.

Be Able to Just Go With The Flow

Never attempt to go against the grain. Day trading is similar to cutting meat. When you are going against the grain, you will find that it's increasingly hard to cut through. Likewise, if you're not careful, you may destroy everything just the same. Think about this thoroughly if you are still a newbie who is looking for a way through. Concentrate on those stocks that sell high and then sell the ones that do not. The reason for this is that stocks normally rise and develop. By using such strategy, you are placing yourself on the safe side.

Be Able to Keep Your Cool and Be Objective

Day trading for beginners would require that you keep your cool at all times and that you try to be as objective as you can in the duration of the entire course. It's but normal that emotions would run high particularly during the rise and fall of such stocks within the day. Be calm. Never allow your emotions to get the better of you which can lead to faulty trading decisions. Be able to assess the situation with much care and never panic. Instead, analyze where you have gone wrong and then pick it up from that point. Learn how to be open and flexible in order for you to easily shift gears when needed.

Remember that Patience is a Requirement and Not Just a Virtue

Bear in mind that things do not always go in such a way that you want them or expect them to. At least, not as soon as you have planned them. Learn to be patient in reaching certain points. It would take you some time and practice to be able to learn the signs on how you could discern if a certain item has reached the peak price. Day trading, as a whole, is not for everyone. If you're the type who is impatient and gets frustrated easily, this type of endeavor may not be a good fit for you. But those who have the perseverance and the readiness to take the fall every now and then can gain much in the financial trading market. Never cease to look for better methods and strategies in reading the signals about when you should buy and sell. You should be able to learn the intricacies involved in the trade by participating in online forums and searching for other useful resources. Before you realize it, you will soon see yourself trading like a pro. Naturally, in order to begin trading like a pro, you should be aware of the pitfalls and snares that should be avoided.